MW01504666

Activities DIY Without Sex

25 exercises for growing love, bliss & intimacy in relationship between creative spiritual women and men

Kash Momo & Moorea Karim

Ecstatic Creation Media LLC

1. Introduction

Figure 1. Purpose of Life is Love, Bliss and Joy ?

Rumi Says:
"We are born of love. Love is our mother."

Are you ready for some action? If not, you will be! If yes, then you will enjoy it!

This entire book is about enjoyable and entertaining activities. This journey contains a selection of highly interesting activities. The purpose of these fun activities is to learn how to experience the optimal arousal of your beingness. You will be easily directed through detailed instructions on how to apply the information provided in this book. Let me give you an example of a little child who loves to dream about how it feels to play all the time. Yes, the same passion is delivered through this book to help you in playing as you continue to imagine the gifts you will receive by the end of this beautiful journey.

What are human needs? Air, water, food, clothes and shelter! You are right, human beings need all this, but they crave something deeper, richer, and more magical. We all love to listen to the stories we used to listen to in our childhood and as an adult, we continue listening to the stories of others. The question is, regardless of the number of stories we listen to each day, why do we still crave something else?

The most appropriate answer to give here is despite our age, gender, and upbringing, we are a soul that craves for being in one another's story. In the modern age, this craving is a constant battle for us that we win through dating, successful outcomes, and finally finding a soul mate who supports us, appreciates us, and keeps our hearts alive more than ever. The spark of youth is determined by the quality of our dating process and relationships. No need to think about your last or any unsuccessful date and relationship, focus on the date and relationship in which you asked yourself are you happy? And the answer that came up was yes, no or maybe? Probably this happens rarely so that your answer is definitely YES. Recall your many dating and relationship experiences? It usually begins with physical attractiveness and ends very soon. Many times, this happens when there is a deprivation of food for your soul and spirit because the relationship cannot provide it.

There is an invisible bond between twins, right? The same kind of emotional bonding and mental compatibility is deeply required for two people who decide to merge with each other. They need to supply their hearts with great awareness about their lives' purpose and visions. This will create a spell to tightly bind them together. This powerful binding spell only works for those people who already have that bright light shining through for them. To let that glowing light out and attract that special someone to be in our story, this book is created for you. It discusses activities that work effectively for this purpose.

As a patron of this book, you will be benefited in many ways. You are free to choose the suitable timing and place for practicing this art by yourself or with your partner. It is easy to follow activities that are presented in this book with simple and thorough instructions that direct you to enhance your attractiveness in your life journey. Secondly, the activities contain variations and options to apply them on with your partner, romantic or what not. You will have more fun things to do. This book's activities also increase your awareness. So that you can more easily evaluate your life based on what you feel, how you feel and why you feel at the core of your heart. It will be a fruitful foundation to optimize your health, pleasure, and bliss.

If yes then right now place your right hand on your heart and take an oath that you will empower yourself with an efficient, time-saving, and cost-effective solution.

Say this aloud:

"I am ready to place my hands on the right person not only claiming to be my partner and also soulmate. I am becoming the right person for my partner and my soulmate too. I am proving it by improving upon myself. I will do it for my partner, with my current partner or future partner. Let it be So. Let it be Done "

Moorea The Author says:
"I want to share my personal experience with you.
I met my beloved Kash after I integrated some tested and proven activities from this book within 3 months of my dating period. After my initial dates with Kash, we did many activities described in this book each time we met. The activities are such well-thought-out resources that give us so much fun and a sense of connectedness. These activities enable us to be more mindful and aware and deepen our bonding. Now we are engaged. Now waiting for our wedding day and as a full-time author, we still love to enjoy the activities very much. Moreover, the variations of activities we develop after we get together are magical. The main goal we achieve through this is enlightening our daily boring routines and breaking the cycle of thoughts and actions like we have had before, such as watching Netflix or YouTube mindlessly. Every time we do the activities together, we feel the growth in our closeness and intimacy. This continues to prevent many unpredictable issues between us due to miscommunication and external causes. We can feel much more with each other compared to our past relationships."

Not only myself, Moorea, my friends, and family also have great results from activities from this book. Below is my best cousin Kevin's testimonial after using the materials from this book.

Kevin says: " I describe myself as an introvert, a tech industry worker who has always been frustrated about my romantic lives. Moorea shares with me a couple of the activities she learned from her relationship retreat in a family gathering. They are really fun and such an authentic way of building genuine connections with others. Then one day, I went to a birthday party for a mutual friend of my current partner. I taught the group a couple of the connection building activities which I learned from Moorea. My partner and I feel the connection in one of the activities and we start dating each other. After 6 months we decided to move in together."

If you have NOT met your partner, this book will help him or her to show up in your reality. Your twin flame, a soul mate, is not far from you anymore. The chapters in this book are carefully organized for you to move in the right direction to connect with the right person. Time doesn't wait for anyone. Today is the day to take the first step and an important one that initiates you on the stage of life where souls meet. You possibly have wasted a lot of youthful years of your life. Every year we heard the news of young celebrities who passed away. They might have left behind their lovers or spouses even if they were planning for their honeymoon or first baby. There are countless incidents of young people passing away reported in the news every year. This is a fact that your tenure on earth is time-limited and unpredictable. It is urgent to spend just 15-20 minutes per day continuously for at least the next 30 days to practice the materials in this book. The investment of your most valuable resource TIME will upgrade your being. It will empower you with heightened mindfulness, awareness, and intuition. This is an easy, affordable and high pay off investment. It will enhance your energy level and make you have a more balanced life. Today is the day to set a goal that is optimally calculated, tried, and true rather than a misaligned goal or brainwashing social media that puts barriers to self-growth and development.

A human is whole with a soulmate as it is written in the story of Adam and Eve in the first chapter of the Bible. Yet modern lifestyle makes finding a soulmate much challenging by introducing the concept of dating. Indeed, dating is a risky investment. You might have remembered how you have wrongly invested emotionally, mentally, physically, and financially in your past relationships. Every time you suffer from dating experience, you become less willing to invest emotionally, financially, mentally, and physically especially when you are hoping for a soulmate but your date is NOT. You might have considered going to a relationship or dating retreat or seminar and yet your resources and circumstances might not allow you to do so. Then this is another reason this book is for YOU.

Almost all the activities in this book are inspired by relationship healing retreats that the authors have attended. Participants attend such retreats for their personal growth and development consciously or out of that unconscious longing of having a soulmate partner. Mostly this type of retreat costs $200USD plus for a single day. A week-long retreat can cost over $1000USD, not including the travel expenses. You have earned yourselves for at least $1000 by buying this book which is full of retreat activities.

If you pick any one of the activities and make it a routine habit to practice consistently for at least 30 days, you will upgrade your self-awareness and intuition to the next level. You might also experience a great flow of energy within your body. You might remember your dreams more clearly and have vivid dreams more frequently or even lucid dreams.

Imagine a stream of bright white light spiraling in the curve of golden ratio above your head. This light enters your head and gradually and slowly moves through your body. This light gradually and slowly transforms into the rainbow. These seven unique colors one by one pass through the whole body of yours. This rainbow charges up your organs, tissues, cells, and atoms. As this rainbow increases in the intensity of brightness moment by moment from the top of your head to the tip of your toes, your cells are happier and happier. Your cells are so happy and blissful. Your cells start smiling, laughing, and singing to you. You smile back to this rainbow and your cells with Love and Gratitude. You can have a lucid dream like that if you practice the material in this book consistently on a regular daily basis.

This is the other purpose of this book, to empower you with tools to tap into the ever-renewing source of energy of the universe as described in ancient spiritual tradition, which has been recently verified by modern science. This ability is our birthright as humans. So, let's exercise this right and privilege as humans. Let's heal ourselves and upgrade our being with this energy to the next level.

After the Corona Virus lockdown, many couples at home have become increasingly bored with one another.This is shown in the divorce rate, which has dramatically skyrocketed compared to that of previous years. Many of these couples got sucked into mindless mainstream media and social media platforms. Don't you know that subliminal brainwashing is embedded in advertising on social media and mainstream media, and have agendas that might not serve our purposes? It can bring us more harm than good. In fact, Silicon Valley's wealthy families have set a very tight limit for the exposure of technology and social media for their young children. These people know what's up and give us a hint. Why wouldn't we spend more time with ourselves and significant others for personal growth, mutual understanding, and genuine connection instead?

To sum up, we feel wholeheartedly that we have benefited so much from practicing the materials in this book. We feel that many people will also benefit, be happier and more blissful from practicing these materials. So, we decided to write this book and share what we have learned, practiced and experienced. Our goal is for anyone to use material from this book to embark on a new journey of life and love. As a result, we hope a happier and more blissful state of humanity will blossom.

The mission of this book is for our readers to experience all of the activities. It would take about 21 days if you and your partner try one activity per day. After experimenting with all the activities in the book, you and your partner would benefit from making a routine out of the activities and sticking with it continuously for another 30 days. You and your partner will be transformed for the better. We wish you an amazing dose of heart-warming success as you discover new levels of Love, Joy and Bliss. Be our patron and see you inside.

2. Heart Basics For Growing A Blissful Relationship

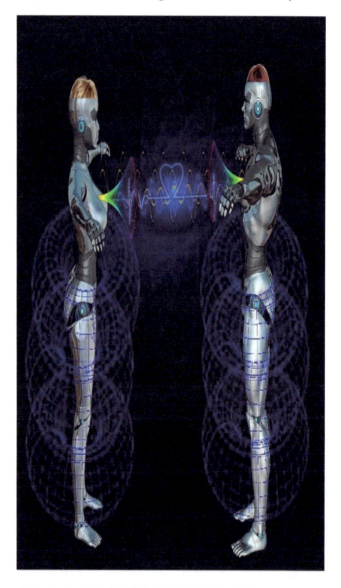

Figure 2. Our Heart produces the biggest magnetic fields which draws events to us..

Rumi Says: "Your Heart is the size of an ocean. Go find yourself in its hidden depths."

Chapter two is the utmost important chapter of upping your relationship to the next level by familiarizing yourself with the science and art of manifestation. If he or she has NOT shown up yet, how could you manifest your partner's soulmate? I.e. How could you manifest yourself into your partner's life? We are what we think. Life experiences shape our behavior. To comply with our beliefs, we feel and act accordingly. The number "TWO" is an enchantment. It represents the female and male that creates all forms in space time. So does this chapter!

What do we think?
Human beings have cognitive functioning that develops throughout life. We act in the same way as we learn. We learn through our caregivers in early childhood years. Our perception was collecting all the information we have today. All the time our mind stores a large amount of sensory information without our awareness in the unconscious mind.

While taking an example of my close friends Miss Tina and Mr. John, who were happily married, but suddenly experienced some arguments that emerged between them about their professional lives in the very first year of their marriage. Tina believed that John would never understand the nature of her job as an interior designer and John demanded her to quit her job as soon as possible after she became pregnant. In retrospect, Tina and John were programmed by the experiences of their parents and manifested similar experiences. Tina's mother told her many times that most husbands will demand his wife to quit her job to be a full-time housewife sooner or later. This is the case for Tina's mother. John has seen his father yelling at his mother because of her job and witnessed many times his father express insecurity and inferiority because his mother earned more than his father. Not a coincidence, Tina earns more than John. They both were already injected with the reasoning and thinking processes behind their conflict before it happened.

Quantum Experiment

Experiments from quantum physics have proved that there is no such thing as objective reality. The young's experiment and its variations have confirmed these over and over. These demonstrations suggest that we, human beings, are the creators of our reality. Our reality is based on what we think, which leads to how we feel, which leads to what we do, which leads to who we are. This means we, as self-sovereign beings, in theory, can choose who we want to be. We are free to choose what we want to think, what we want to feel, what we want to do and who we want to be. We are the magnets or repellant for anything in our life including our partners, soulmates, and lovers. We are projecting the shape, color, and quality of them from ourselves. We are imagining them to be.

Let's use a metaphor. "Two bodies and one soul." This statement can be imagined by placing a knife between a burning candle flame. This knife divides the flame into two. In fact, they are still one. The knife that has been stopping you from actualizing the love of your life is the way you think. The need is to turn that knife into a thread and let that thread burn so that all fake barriers vanish. Among the infinite possibilities of the universe, your soulmate already exists. You just have to manifest your soulmate. You can attract your soulmate with your heart. Then, two hearts, that are yearning for each other, can now melt, fuse and merge into one in apparent and actuality.

Holographic Universe

Have you ever heard that we are living in a hologram? Another mind-provoking idea of science described by physicists is the holographic nature of our universe in which we are living. This holographic principle states that every single part of the universe contains all the information needed to re-create the whole universe. Interesting right? Without digging deep into the complex details of the subject, we can see that this same principle goes with our thought processes. In fact, many studies indicate that our brain is holographic in nature. As it says: "As above, so below. "

We are in the Matrix.

Research shows that we alter our memory based on how we feel and interpret our memory. Similarly, we tend to believe in information with or without evidence based on our previous experiences, learning and programing. This lines up with the case of John and Tina once again. It is easy for the human mind to think a certain way, so long the mind has been thinking that way in routine. This gives us quick and effortlessly automatic thinking and living. Doesn't it sound wonderful, perhaps like a robot? This is a fortune and an unfortunate design. Remember these sayings:" Ignorance is Bliss." "Fool me once, shame on you. Fool me twice, shame on me." This is indeed a double-edged sword. It is the cutting edge and the bleeding edge.

Take some time to recall the story line in the Movie Matrix. Neo eventually figures it out. He learns and masters the art of how to change the holographic reality by changing his mind. The philosophical concept raised by Descartes, a French mathematician, discussed the uniqueness of human beings. It is because of our minds that we are able to reflect, think about past experiences objectively, and make decisions and adjustments. I think, therefore I am. The higher brain functions give us our free choice to choose options available to us. We have the freedom to solve a problem through intellectual autonomy in any situation. This ability is not only about wisdom and intelligence level. It requires the art and skill of utilizing the information around us through intuitions. Focusing on possible solutions and an alternative favorable outcome is our birthright as a human. Other creatures can only focus on known predictable consequences from previous programming. Human beings have a complex brain structure. The frontal lobe of our brain is the most developed and complex among all creatures on Earth. It lets us self-regulate our behaviors. It lets us be creative and seek guidance from our past experiences. Thanks to the hippocampus, all the programming and memories of past events are carefully placed and resting there. We have the choice to replace any painful and unsuccessful memories and programming with productive and happy ones if we choose to. We can shift from failure to success.

Mimic Neurons and Brain Waves

Mimic neurons indicate the importance of any external role model that one can mimic. The Mimic neurons copy and make sense of the events and signals generated by the role model. The ingesting of signals is much more significant, formative and active in our early childhood. It is because during that period, the state of the brain waves are alpha and theta. These states allow information and stimuli from our environment to constantly and easily embed into the unconscious. These memories and programming form the core of our behavior system. Many studies show that when a child witnesses domestic violence, as an adult he or she will usually fail to relate with a partner romantically. It is because mimic neurons make us mimic the behavior we have learned in the past. When we enter adulthood, our brain wave circuitry is dominated by beta which shelters the unconscious. As a result, once we become adults, it is challenging to change unless we consciously choose to alter this programming with our free will.

The Concept of Change

The good news is that changing our behavior and attitude with ourselves and/or with our partners is possible. We can behave in any manner we choose in any circumstance and situation, provided that enough training is taken. The behaviors we exhibit are triggered by the stored information and memories in our unconscious mind. They are outside our conscious awareness, but it is possible to replace them with the use of visualization and imagination. The brain and mind don't know the difference between real events and powerful imaginary events. Your imagination is powerful enough to hack your brain. In this way, you have the power to change your behavior. You have the power to attract anything into your life, including a new lover, soulmate or twin flame.

Spiritual Tradition vs. Modern Science

There are four levels of human intelligence based on a spiritual healer and scholar of ancient times. Renowned world teacher Sadhguru Jaggi Vasudev concludes that our identity is what we construct about ourselves with the use of our thoughts and beliefs. Spiritual traditions also emphasize the tremendous power of the untapped potential of our unconscious mind as well as unseen energy fields governing the analytical functioning of our conscious mind and measurable physical energy.

Today, scientists suggest that our cosmos consists of 85% dark matter and 68% dark energy. In modern science, it says that the unconscious mind is linked with our bodily sensations and intelligence at the cellular level. It implies that we can reach out to the unconscious mind through sensual experience. When this is possible, we can heal our emotions, replace our habits, change our character and bring forth an upgraded version of ourselves. We have enormous potential as humans. We have the power to be the person we are dreaming of becoming.

The Importance of the Heart

The heart pumps out about 2 ounces of blood every time our heart beats. At least 2,500 gallons of blood are pumped daily in our body. The heart can beat over 3 billion times in a person's life. In 1991, scientists found that there are 40k neuron cells in the heart. The heart can feel, learn, sense and remember, as a little brain. In fact, our heart produces the largest and strongest magnetic field among all organs. Do you know all wild creatures can predict natural disasters in advance? Research finds that the feelings of love and gratitude induce heart-brain coherence. The brain and heart sync up at a frequency of about 7-8 HZ, which is the frequency of mother earth. When our heart and brain are in coherence, we link up and communicate with the whole universe via mother earth. Ancient spiritual tradition says that humans have the same ability to predict natural disasters, just like wild creatures do, the abilities are just latent. As stories from mystics and sages suggest, we as humans have the potential to have communion with the whole of creation and beyond.

Avatar: The Movie

In the Hollywood movie, Avatar, a popular message was shared. It is applicable to all humanity. It is to honor the sacred, love, and the heart. This exemplifies beautifully that seeking love and returning it is our natural human condition. According to David Wilcock, all Hollywood hit movies have the obvious and not so obvious agenda of propagating ideas that the creator wants us to embody. We can be the avatars of our lives. From the research of Heart Math Institute and many others, it concludes that we need a coherent heart and coherent brain in order to manifest. Let's see how it works in practice.

Now use your most vibrant creative juice to write a script for yourself and your partner of how you can up level your heart connection with oneself and one another. Spend at least 10 minutes and let your imagination go wild. Then, go to the suggested exercises scripts chapter to see what we have for you.

Now. Scribble with your hands or your mind's eye. Enjoy!

3. Love Thyself And Flow With Your Partner

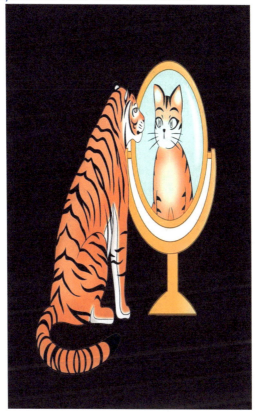

Figure 4. We see what We believe.

Charlie Chaplin says:" The mirror is my best friend because when I cry it never laughs."

Rumi says: "As you live Deeper in the Heart, the Mirror gets clearer and cleaner."

Let's review the key concepts in the last chapter.

Heart:

Our heart is the number one hard-working muscle in the whole human body. It generates an electromagnetic field which is about 60 times bigger in amplitude compared to that of the brain. As a result, it produces the strongest rhythmic field of the human body. Moreover, scientists find that when the brain and heart are in sync, it arrives at the frequency of about 7-8 Hz which is equal to the earth's frequency. As a result, the coherence of the brain and heart builds a communication link between the human body and Mother Earth. Research suggests that Earth also communicates with other planets and systems in the universe. As a result, when our hearts and brain are in-sync, we communicate with the whole of creation.

We Are What We Believe:

Nature, nurture, genetics, and environment determine what we believe and who we are. They make us think, feel, and act in certain ways. Our values and beliefs are dictated by the company we keep, especially during our formative years. As a result, we make choices and take actions similar to those of our parents and caretakers both consciously and unconsciously. We decide to do one thing and to quit another. The color we love, the music we listen to, the profession we choose and the partner we love are all the products of our actions triggered by our beliefs.

Your Universe Exists Because Of You.

You are the most important character in your story. If your character ceases to exist, then YOUR universe ceases to exist as there is NO MORE YOU. As a result, the higher self favors you all the time and you don't even know it. It can turn your disappointments into a happy and blissful future provided that you give the correct direction. You give direction all the time, mostly through sensations, consciously and unconsciously. The universe wants to make you HAPPY. It is your right for the arrival of a soul mate if you desire it. It can happen sooner than you expect with the personality and qualities that you desire. This is your birthright. Visualize and Feel the sensation, cherish and receive it with gratitude and live it Now, every moment and forevermore!

Mirror WHO?

The mirror is our image of the self. We only see in others what we have in ourselves. What we find in our world is the projection of our inner state. Suppose a partner of yours is exactly what you want him or her to be, consciously and unconsciously. In the same way, our dating behaviors and the treatment our partner shows is the projection of their personality and inner world. How and what they see in us, and how they value us is their reality coming straight from the unconscious dimension of mind. We trigger them to behave in the way they do. They manifest what they have inside their hearts.

The ONE agreement

In his book, The Four Agreements, Don Miguel Ruiz requests his students not to take anything personally in any situation. He says that the person acts, feels and thinks according to his or her manufactured reality. This manufactured reality is created from his or her beliefs. For example, a realized saint, like Gautama the Buddha, has followers as well as critics and enemies, like Devadatta. A dictator like Hitler has both followers as well as buddies, like Hermann Göring. There is always someone in the universe who agrees or disagrees with any of the ideas you have.

Who tells the TRUTH?

The most accurate predictor of truth is probably through our unconscious mind. For example, numerous experiments have demonstrated that physical reactions including pulse, pupil dilation, and brain wave activities change between 1 to 10 seconds before an individual sees a horrifying photograph (Example: a realistic photoshopped picture of a tiger mauling a human in a Hollywood movie). In all of these experiments, horrifying pictures are mixed randomly with serene pictures. (Example: the Himalaya mountain). The conscious minds of participants have no idea of which photograph would be shown next, but their unconscious mind does.

Another example is from a news story in January 2018. A man from Virginia, USA named Victor Amole dreamed about the numbers 3-10-17-26-32 very vividly. He had never had a vivid dream with numbers like that in his whole life, up to that point in time. As a result, he was very curious and chose to enter the lottery with those numbers. More interestingly, He was so confident that he bought four lottery tickets with those numbers. Amazingly, he won. Each ticket was worth USD 100000. To win that lottery with five arbitrary numbers, the probability was 1 out of 278,256. Ancient spiritual tradition suggests that our unconscious mind knows everything across space and time, provided that one can tap into it and express it in a tangible and understandable way in the conscious dimension. Fortunately, and unfortunately, few human beings have this ability.

Now use your most vibrant creative juice to write a script for yourself and your partner of how you can up level your own understanding with oneself using a mirror and your partner. Spend at least 10 minutes and let your imagination go wild. Then, go to the suggested exercises scripts chapter to see what we have for you.

Now. Scribble with your hands or your mind's eye. Enjoy.

4. Grow Kindness Through Eyes Of Your Partners

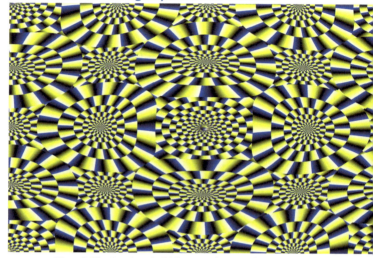

Figure 5. What is seeing what? My eyes, my brain or what?

As of 2020 May, on the internet site recordsetter.com says Julio J. kept his eyes open without blinking for one hour, five minutes, 11.46 seconds. Try Not blinking and stare at the above image for one minute at a distance about when you are taking a selfie.

Have you ever watched a show involving a hypnotherapist who uses a pendulum to capture a person's gaze and trigger a self-generated deep trance? Many times while in a trance state, the person can demonstrate a feat that is NOT possible in their normal waking state. Our inner eyes can be a gateway to power for manifestation. Coupled with our bodily sensations and emotions, they can manifest our dreams into reality. It works if we allow ourselves to feel what we want from the core of our being in the unconscious body sensation level, in every moment.

Eyes are the windows to the soul and undoubtedly, they reveal our emotional state. They give way to reveal our mind and brain's processing. Recall an eye gaze of a loving partner. Recall an eye gaze of an abusive partner. How does it feel differently? Your gaze changes with your internal state. You might gaze to the left, right, top, or bottom unconsciously. You know, our left brain communicates what we perceive from the left eye and vice versa. Our eye is the only organ that does not use cross over communication with our brain. Ancient yogic practices suggest that the direction of eye gaze can be used to alter our internal state. Modern science suggests similar possibilities. Past researches suggest that our right brain is more of the creative oriented processing. It controls the left side of the body. Similarly, the right side of the body is controlled by the left region of the brain which is geared more toward analytical thinking. It deals with types of processing such as arithmetic and reality-based thinking, like recalling an event. However, recent research shows that our brain works more as a whole unit of neural networks, despite the different regions being activated for different activities. Next time, pay attention to if your eyes look one way or the other when you are recalling an event or doing something creative. Gautama the Buddha says only trust our personal experience and conviction. We, the authors, agree with this saying completely. Certain Tibetan Buddhist meditation techniques state that gazing into space with diverse focus can create profound bliss and deep trance. We, the authors, while embarking on a psychedelic mushroom journey, did that practice and it worked. Later on, we tried without the mushrooms and it still worked, but the bliss was less intense. Give it a try with or with some boost.

What else does modern research say?

Do you know that vision activates about two-thirds of the electrical activity in the brain? In 1957, a scientific study was published in a paper by a neuroanatomist named R.S. Fixot who discovered this fact. When we open our eyes, the neurons in the visual cortex of our brain fire at a rate of 2-3 billion per second. This translates to our eyes consuming 40% of all the processing power of our brain. Moreover, nerve fibers in our retina have direct connections to our brains. Based on these facts, we can say that the neural tissues for our vision are the most prominent among other sensory neural tissues.

Statistics regarding nerve fibers in human eyes are also quoted in Eric Jensen's book. In his book titled, *Brain-Based Learning*, he explained visual learning processes. He wrote the same information as that of the paper validated in an American journal of ophthalmology. Directly or indirectly, they cited that our neural tissues are highly biased towards vision, and as a result, visual learning can be the most efficient among other styles of learning.

For most people, if they can only keep one sense, sight is the one. We learn a lot about our partner through vision. We've all heard of the saying, "Love at first sight". Most of our neurons are dedicated to vision, as compared to the other four senses of hearing, smell, taste, and touch. When making decisions, the other four senses are not equal to the power of vision, even if they work together collectively. Our vision is out-evolving our sense of sound, smell, taste, and touch..

Another book written by John Medina called, *Brain Rules,* tells the story of the evolutionary matches between sight and sound. In the early mammalian days,the senses of sound and sight were quite equal in power. As we know, many mammals have a keener sense of sound than of sight, and many mammals have limited color vision compared to humans. When humans came along, there was a match between the two senses for activating the highest share of neurons and processing power in the brain. Eventually, the visual cortex wins this match. With the latest upgrade of our brain's neural cortex, especially the frontal lobe, humans became sight-orientated. We have the power of self-reflection of the NOW and to experience self-regulation of our PRESENT and future behavior. This is a real breakthrough in Mother Earth's creation.

Egyptian and Cat

Egyptians know that cats have very top-notch psychic abilities compared to other animals. As a result, the cat was worshiped back then and even now amongst many cat lovers. Cats know when someone is about to pass away, as many stories have been told in elderly homes and auspices. Cats have amazing intuition compared to most domesticated animals. They sense like wild animals. Humans have this ability too, as many stories from Aboriginal people of the land have verified. We, the authors, have a cat and have experienced many magical incidents with our cat. Notice how enchanting a cat's eyes are next time you come across onet. You can bring this magic into your life through your eyes too.

Now use your most vibrant creative juice to write a script for yourself and your partner of how you can up level your own understanding with oneself using your eyes and your partner's eyes. Spend at least 10 minutes and let your imagination go wild. Then, go to the suggested exercises scripts chapter to see what we have for you.

Now. Scribble with your hands or your mind's eye. Enjoy!

5. Grow Intimacy By Tuning Into Your Partner's Field

Figure 6. www.JediSchool.science

The Authors say: "May the Source be with you"

Guess who is that legendary fictional character that is short in stature like a Midget, green like stinging nettle, has verbal dyslexia, has big pointy ears worse than those of a mutated kangaroo and yet is the most revered master in the whole universe. You are correct! "Yoda!" The master Jedi from the 1980's "THE STAR WARS UNIVERSE". One of the Yoda quotes is, "A Jedi uses the Force for knowledge and defense, never for attack".

This chapter will talk about the biofield and one of the best practices to energize and enlarge your biofield through Tai Chi Zhang Zhong. You may become healthier and more vibrant if you keep this practice as a routine habit. One thing leads to another, you might be very charismatic compared to the obsolete version of your old self. You might be able to seduce the opposite sex much easier compared to the outdated version of your old self, so be cautious if you already have a partner. Remember what master Yoda has taught us. We should only use our upgraded good vibes for the greater good.

What is the Bio-Field?

In 1994, a group of scientists at the National Institute of Health invented the term Bio-field. In human interactions and healing applications, it signifies the underlying human energy field or aura. All living organisms contain this field of information.

Bio-field from the perspective of Yoga

On the contrary, we have some of the very interesting traditional lessons from yogis who have practiced meditation. In their deep meditation, these yogis have realized that there are many layers of human existence. Using modern analogy, we can say there are five of them.

1. The hardware, the physical body, is called Annamaya Kosha, which is a literal translation of "the food body".
2. The mind-body software is called Manomaya Kosha.
3. The power source, the energy body, is called Pranamaya Kosha.
4. The bridge between space-time (physical) bodies of the above three to the body that is beyond space-time, is the wisdom body. It is called the Vijnanamaya Kosha.
5. The last and final layer, the bliss body, is called Anandamaya Kosha.
6. The bliss body only has a tiny separation between an individual entity and the SOURCE. This body is the real user of this virtual real character we call oneself.

Pranmayama, one of the main practices in Yoga, is controlled breathing exercise. The main aim is to develop the Pranamaya Kosha, the energy body. Rhythmic breathing is one of the most basic forms of pranayama. The human biofield is the scientific counterpart of the yogic concept of Pranamaya Kosha. According to research, illness arises when the frequency of the human bio-field decreases from a certain desirable level, or the field itself is out of balance. You might have heard or observed that a group of pendulums in proximity will eventually move in sync. It also happens with biological systems. Perhaps you remember the last time you felt energized and refreshed after going out into nature and camping for a few days. Your body's bio-field had been synced-up to and re-balanced by the biggest bio-field– nature from Mother Earth.

The bio-field can be the main reason behind why we're motivated to move somewhere or feel attracted to someone. The bio-field of that particular location or human being can be complementary and have beneficial effects with our own. There are many documented stories which describe how after an organ transplant, the behaviors of the receiver change dramatically. The organ receiver would pick up the same likings and dislikings of the organ donor. As an organ contains the field of information of the owner's, we may deduce that the bio-field is one of the major influencers of our behavior.

Atom's Story

The most fundamental unit of the universe is the atom. The recent scientific experiment shows that an atom is conscious in the way that it behaves according to the observer's expectation. Scientists suggest that 99.9999999% of an atom consists of space. This space is not empty. This space is a field filled with an energy called Zero Point Energy.

The distance between the atom's nucleus and its electron is comparatively vast. To illustrate this concept, imagine a baseball floating in the sky. Its electron will orbit in a sphere with a radius of 25 km. It is quite mind-blowing!

The story continues...

We, humans, tend to form family, extended family and community up to the level of the entire country and beyond, right? Atoms are doing the same thing. A few atoms get together and bond together and form a molecule. The atoms within the molecule share information or energy among each other via the overlapping field occupied by their electrons. For example, we have the water molecule H_2O. Next level up, molecules can band together and form complex chemicals such as Aspirin $C_9H_8O_4$. Getting more and more complex now, we have amino acids, the proteins that are the fundamental units of Organic Life forms on Earth.

Atom's story with the Bio-field

If you imagine the human body as a spaceship, we can say that it is made out of many systems. For example, the respiratory system has bronchi and lungs to make the breathing process possible. There are other systems such as the digestive system, nervous system, and reproductive system. Any of these systems are made out of specific organs which in turn are made out of very specific tissues. For example, the tissue in your reproductive system is very different from the tissue in your elimination system, even though they are neighbors of each other. The tissues are made out of cells. The cell is a biological molecule containing many other molecules, namely, proteins, lipids, carbohydrates, and nucleic acids. These proteins, complex chemicals, and chemicals are made out of molecules that are made out of atoms. So, we can say that Humans are made out of atoms just like anything else in the Observable Universe.

As there is a field of energy and information permeating amongst all the atoms, we can theorize that there is a field of energy and information permeating the human body too. This field of energy and information has been documented in many ancient spiritual practices like the Indian Yogic system and the Chinese Chi Gong system. Notice that the bio-field has been recently verified and documented by modern science. For example, Dr. Hiroshi Motoyama developed the Apparatus for Meridian Identification to measure the energy of the Chinese Meridian system. Dr. Konstantin Korotkov developed the Bio-well system to measure the Biofield via measuring Biophotons.

Just like any human-made organization has its mission statement and protocol of communication, the human organism has the biofield for information and energy exchanges among its members. And the most fundamental statement is to exist and survive as an individual and to reproduce offspring so that the species as a whole also survives. This implies that at any moment, if our identity of being ourselves is being threatened, it creates stress as it is against the prime directive of our organism.

What do we learn from Dr. Joe Dispenza?

Have you ever been in a stressful situation?? Example: You are in a very bad traffic jam and your colon and rectum are FULL. You need to relieve yourself or else you'll literally SHIT your UNDERPANTS!! What would you be thinking?? This has happened to me before, so I know. When will I get out?? Where will I find a toilet?? So, it implies that our consciousness is gearing toward the observation of space and time. As you may know, if a thing is bound by space and time, then this thing is physical. Anything physical is bound by the first law of thermodynamics, which eventually degrades toward chaos and destruction.

Anytime an organism is under stress, it implies that it's in survival mode, which can be categorized by fight, flight, hide and freeze. It corresponds to the fact that stress is the most harmful factor of our well being. And all organisms in nature can only handle a limited amount of stress in short spurs, or else die prematurely. Ancient spiritual practice and modern science agree that our bio-field diminishes whenever we are in stress.

Piezoelectric Effect of Human Bone

Have you wondered why in meditation class they tell you to cross your legs? Ancient Yogic tradition suggests that when our body is held in a certain geometry, it resonates with the field of mother earth to a much higher degree. Modern science has discovered the Piezoelectric Effect of human bone. Human bone can generate an electric charge and electromagnetic field when the bone is subjected to mechanical pressure. Moreover, some research suggests that the entire body behaves as a piezoelectric crystal such as Quartz crystal. This research implies that the human body is a living antenna, like what has been taught in the Ancient Yogic tradition.

Yoda has said, "MAY THE FORCE BE WITH YOU."

Obi-Wan, a grandmaster Jedi, explains the force to his protege Luke like this:

"Well, the Force is what gives a Jedi his power. It's an energy field created by all living things. It surrounds us and penetrates us. It binds the galaxy together."

Does it seem to contradict what Yoda says, if it surrounds us and penetrates us, how could it not be with us?

It can be interpreted like this.

"May you embody the Force in its ultimate degree of Purity, Purpose, and Power. " If we are indeed living antennae, it is possible that we have corrupted our geometry and material composition knowingly or unknowingly."

Yet, Mother Nature is gracious and full of Love and compassion. We can always bring ourselves back to harmony and be in the flow with the bio-field, THE FORCE.

Let us relax through the activities given in this chapter to tune up and energize our bio-field. This tuned-up, energized and endowed biofield will attract our optimized partner from a box of souls, like blossoming flowers to bees, and repels the non-optimized ones like holy water for vampires. You might very much feel like you knew your partners before you two met. You two's bio-fields might have communicated in vast distances already via your bio-field human antennas.

Now use your most vibrant creative juice to write a script for yourself and your partner of how you can up level your own force field and your partner's. Spend at least 10 minutes and let your imagination go wild. Then, go to the suggested exercises scripts chapter to see what we have for you.

Now. Scribble with your hands or your mind's eye. Enjoy!

6. Grow Intimacy Using Your Partner's Energy Vortexes

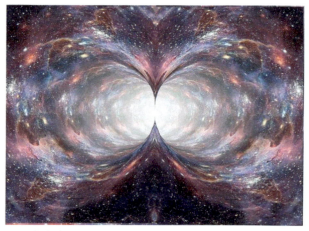

Figure 7. The fundamental building block of the Universe is a Torus ?.

Nikola Tesla said:

"If we want to find the secrets of the universe, think in terms of energy, frequency and vibration"

Moorea the author says: "Have you ever noticed that there are some places where we feel energetic and at some other places, we feel lethargic for no reason? Even if we are completely rested, the places have some kind of vibes that draw our energy and mood down. For example, at my previous job, Mary, Winnie, and I shared the same office room where we rarely talk to each other. However, once we stepped out of the office room, we got along very well. We could spend hours talking about random things in the office café. Our favorite topic is gossiping though LoL."

Recap from the previous chapter: Science suggests that our body is aware consciously and unconsciously all the time. We are heavily influenced by the energy, frequency, and vibration that surrounds us. All of this energy, frequency and vibration is being picked up by our body consciously or unconsciously. All of this energy, frequency and vibration is then turned into signals that influence us. These signals travel via our spinal cord and nerves to every cell of our body.

In fact, the Ancient Yogic tradition states that there are power centers called Chakras present in our body that share and exchange information with the universe. Remember in previous chapters, we discussed 5 layers of bodies, some of which are not located in this physical dimension. Similarly, the power centers are not all in this physical dimension. However, the major power centers are located along our spinal cord when they are in this physical dimension. In his book, *Eyes of Lotus*, Dr.

Richard Jelusich, a psychic, describes that a Chakra is a vortex, shaped like a donut, in which the axis of spin is along our spinal cord. In fact, Chakra means 'wheel' in Sanskrit. Our Chakras are our energy vortexes in this mini-universe we call our body. These chakras have unique characteristics from each other. They each act as a lens and filter for the information that we receive from the universe. For most humans, we are either right-handed or left-handed. Similarly, we have a tendency and preference to use a specific chakra to filter and interpret the information we receive. However, every chakra must not be used in excess. If so, it might result in an imbalance. For example, when a person who is dominated by their throat chakra overuses their throat chakra, the expressive and talkative nature of their personality can create irritations and solicit problems in a relationship. Dr. Hiroshi Motoyama has described two incidents of Chakra overuse in his book: *Theories of the Chakras: Bridge to Higher Consciousness.* An Indian Yogi who was a pranayama expert that could stop his pulse at will and a Filipino psychic who could perform psychic surgery without any tools or anesthesia, are two examples of highly evolved humans who both passed away prematurely in their 50s due to the overuse of their heart chakras.

When correlating these ancient traditions with modern science, it is suggested that each physical chakra corresponds to the major cluster of neurons and glands controlled by the autonomic nervous systems along the spine. Notice that there are seven major chakras and there are seven major glands in the human body.

Root Chakra and Sex Chakra

The first chakra is called root chakra. Dr. Jelusich suggests that the first chakra is the gateway of the soul, manifested into the physical dimension. The first chakra corresponds to the most basic survival instincts one has as an individual.

Moorea, the Author says: "My grandma tells me her experience when she was in China. Her family raised pigs for food. Whenever they would slaughter a pig for a feast, they would always put the pig into a bamboo cage and drown it in water. As the pig was being drowned, it would freak out and all its urine and feces would spew out of its body." Similarly, one would pee or shit in their pants when they're in extreme fear for their survival. There is no clear cut answer for this behavior from scientific points of view. However, from the theory of chakras, it makes sense. As the root chakra is the gateway from spiritual to physical,it is in charge of the safety and security of the being as an individual.

The second chakra is called the sex chakra. The second chakra corresponds to the second most basic instincts, a.k.a. sex, which makes an individual survive through offspring. The sex chakra is the feeling chakra. It is the sensual chakra which creates the "feeling" through our five sensory inputs. Indeed, the area around our sex chakra is the most erogenous zone of our body. Before the advances of technology, the best and easiest available form of entertainment for humans was sex. Observing our close cousin chimps and monkey, they do very much enjoy using sex as a form of entertainment. Today, it says that 90% of all internet traffic is Porn or Sex-related. Sex is such an activity that it has all the five senses involved. And the "HIGH" created is such a reward, as it promotes oneself's immortality through the creation of offspring.

Many traditions suggest the root chakras is associated with a deep red color and the sex chakra is a red or orange color. One can use Root vegetables like potatoes, parsnips, radishes, beets, onions, garlic,protein-rich food like eggs, beans, peanuts, or sesame to boost these two chakras. Also, one can also use dark or red crystals such as Red Jasper or Black Tourmaline to cleanse, balance, or activate these chakras. People feel safe, secure, and passionate about life when these two center's energies are balanced and present in adequate amounts.

As a chakra is, in essence, an energy and information center, we can use our conscious mind to program it. For this purpose, the first chakra is located at the midpoint of the perineum. The second chakra is above the pubic bone about three fingers deep inside in the front part of the spine. People who wish to strengthen the root Chakra's functioning usually use the affirmation "I AM" and the emotion and sensation of being secure and safe. People who wish to strengthen the sex Chakra's functioning usually use the affirmation "I FEEL" and the emotion and sensation of passion and excitement.

Navel and Solar Plexus Chakra

The third chakra is called navel chakra or Solar Plexus Chakra. It corresponds to the digestive glands and adrenal glands. This is the energy center for transforming physical food into usable forms of energy for the body. It also controls the fight or flight responses. So, you could also say that the navel chakra is a kind of survival center, similar to the root and sexual chakra. People feel confident and have a feeling of self-worth when the navel chakra's energy is balanced and abundant.

The navel chakra is associated with the color yellow. For boosting these Chakras, one can use food abundant in yellow coloring, such as bananas, pineapple, lemon, and yellow curry. One can also use hemp seed, flaxseed, and sprouted grains. One can also use Amber and Orange Calcite crystals to balance and cleanse this chakra.

The location of Navel Chakra is deep inside the navel on the spine. The location of the Solar Plexus Chakra is at the midpoint between the navel and the tip of the sternum, deep into the stomach. People who wish to strengthen their functioning usually use the affirmation "I CAN" and the emotion and sensation of being empowered and confident.

Heart Chakra

The fourth chakra corresponds to the heart, blood vessels, circulation system and thymus gland. Many traditions acknowledge LOVE as the attribute of the heart. To Love is to give and serve altruistically. It implies that one has to go beyond one's limited small physical self and embrace a self that includes "OTHERS", such as friends, families, communities, countries, mother earth, all the way up to the whole cosmos. People feel happy and joyful when the heart chakra's energy is balanced and abundant.

This chakra is associated with the color green. One can ingest green-colored food such as spinach, dandelion greens, stinging nettle, lamb's quarter, celery, cucumber, zucchini, matcha, green tea, avocado, mint, kiwi, spirulina, or green apple to boost the energy of this chakra. One can also use green crystals such as green Jade, Emerald, and Malachite.

The location of this chakra is simply in our hearts. Note that we can only create something bigger than our small self, after we pass survival mode. As a result, for creating anything significant, we need to have our energy reach and go beyond the Heart Chakra. People who wish to strengthen their Heart Chakra's functioning can use the affirmation "I LOVE", with the emotions and sensations of gratefulness, altruistic giving, serving and well-wishing of OTHERS.

Throat Chakra

The fifth chakra is the throat chakra. It corresponds to the thyroid gland. It is in charge of communication. As we know, any successful communication needs to be two-way and balanced. There has to be a sender and a receiver. Both of these channels have to be open in order to have the communication flowing smoothly. Also, the channels must NOT corrupt the information. In the previous chapter, we talk about how the majority of the energy and matter in this universe is NOT measurable, it is so-called Dark Energy and Dark Matter. In fact, recent studies suggest that verbal communication accounts for only 5 percent of all the information exchange among humans. Much of the information exchanged can be non-physical in nature and occurs in the unconscious realm.

The throat chakra is associated with the color blue. Blueberries can help to balance and cleanse the energy of this chakra. Blue crystals such as Turquoise and Lapis Lazuli can help to balance and cleanse the energy of this chakra. People experience self-actualization through expression and communication when this center's energy is balanced and abundant.

The throat Chakra is located at the pit of the throat, the vertebrae that connects the neck to the torso. People who wish to strengthen its functionality usually use the affirmation, "I OPEN", and feel the emotions and sensations of being TRUTHFUL and HONEST to oneself and others.

Third Eye and Crown Chakra

The sixth chakra is the third eye chakra. The seventh chakra is the crown chakra. The third eye chakra corresponds to the pineal and pituitary gland. Some traditions suggest the crown chakra corresponds with the whole brain's activated state, so there is no ONE physical location. In Sanskrit, crown chakra is called Sahasrara, which translates to, "a thousand-petaled lotus", which corresponds to all the neurons in the brain. Dr. Jelusish suggests that the crown Chakra is a gateway in reverse of that of the Root Chakra. It acts like a black hole that can open our consciousness from the physical to the non-physical, which is beyond space and time.

In Dr. Joe Dispenza's book, *Becoming Supernatural*, his students' whole brain is activated during deep ecstatic meditation. These students are in a high power Gamma brain waves state. During this meditation, the power consumption of the brain is 200 -500 times the standard deviation from that of a normal waking state. Put it into metaphor, it's like observing the height of an average adult human to be 5 feet 8 inches, then finding a freak of nature that is 100 feet tall like King Kong.

Dr. Joe Dispenza also suggests that our pineal gland serves as a transducer that can pick up signals that are non-physical, non-temporal and non-measurable. In the research of Dan Winter, he discusses the conversion of the Transversal EM wave to longitude EM wave through the trajectory of a golden spiral on the surface of a pinecone. Once the EM signal transforms into a longitude wave, the signal can go beyond the space and time continuum. The details of this are out of scope of this book, but the reader is encouraged to do more research. In summary, the implications of these two studies agree with the ancient yogic practice that once the Third Eye Chakra and Crown Chakra get activated, one has the possibility of going beyond space and time.

People who wish to strengthen the third eye chakra and crown chakra and its functioning can just observe SILENCE. Relax, observe Silence and just BE. For the third eye chakra and crown chakra, it is best on fasting or intermittent fasting. Cleansing and Purification is the key. Clear Quartz Crystal and Moldavite can be good crystals to help open these two chakras.

To sum up, Chakras have a great influence on how we think and on our cognitive functioning capacities. They maintain an aura and a field for us. They filter and transform the energy, frequency and vibration from our environment. This filtration and transformation makes us think, feel, act and react in a way that is unique to each one of us. Whenever our energy is balanced, aligned, and resonates with someone, we appreciate them and are happy to be around them. This is nature's way of giving us the signal that someone is compatible with us and may be a candidate for being a soulmate or twin flame.

Figure 8. Major Chakras and their associated hormonal glands

Now use your most vibrant creative juice to write a script for yourself and your partner of how you can tune up your vortex and your partner's. Spend at least 10 minutes and let your imagination go wild. Then, go to the suggested exercises scripts chapter to see what we have for you.

Now. Scribble with your hands or your mind's eye. Enjoy!

7. Deepen Your Relationship With Sound

Figure 9. Why did my parents pull my ears and make me pull my own ears when I was young ?

Diogenes says: "We have two ears and one tongue so that we would listen more and talk less."

When a new soul comes into the world, we look for signs of life. It may be the sound of the air pulled into the lungs or the startled cry he or she makes when getting acquainted with gravity. Besides our physical ears, many spiritual traditions claim that we also have a spiritual ear, which we can tap into if we quiet down, look within and discover things that give us bliss.

Do we really have a spiritual ear?

Have you ever had a panic attack? Sometimes, in mild cases, we call it "monkey brains". We get into a state of anxiety and we have so many trains of thought that we can't concentrate. To get back to mindfulness, we need elements that help quiet the turmoil. Sounds and music can be a good choice for this purpose.

Moorea the author says: "I lived in a girls Co-op when I was in college. There was this girl who had anger issues. Even a little fuss, like someone forgetting to close the window, and she'd blow up and start cursing like there is no tomorrow. One time, I forgot to turn off the oven light and she found out. She became literally NUTS and chased me and cursed me with F-bombs for one hour. She got kicked out two weeks after this incident. However, whenever I would hear anyone that sounds like her, I would have a panic attack. That's how it got me to explore the possibilities on how to use sound to purge this trauma, as this trauma was caused by sound too."

Whenever we are in panic mode, we have lost touch with our spirit and we can't listen to others. Listening is a vital key to communication, the base of everything working right in the world. When we quiet down and listen, energy flows with ease, our bodies relax, and we are open to new possibilities.

This "inner ear" isn't something physical, it is the device that picks up the small still voice from Spirit. The guidance that we all have from birth until DEATH. This inner ear represents the endless possibilities of listening to the silence of our own SELF.

Hearing vs. Listening

Hearing is a sophisticated system that involves the whole body, physically and emotionally. We can hear somebody talk, but sometimes their message doesn't reach the target. The ear has an outer and an inner part, and it is the first element that we develop completely in the womb. This is to be able to connect with the beating heart vibrations of the mother.

The outer layer catches the sound, which is a mix of vibrations that the auditory nerve turns into a code and channels it inside. Here, three bones deliver the package to the brain. Then, the brain proceeds to decipher the message. If we find ourselves in an unbalanced phase, we're not going to be able to listen, we're going to jump to conclusions based on what triggered us from past experiences.

Listening is a skill. We hear many couples complain that their significant others don't listen anymore after a year of living together. This is true. In our busy daily schedules, we forget to take time to relax, reflect, and to practice mindful listening to ourselves and others. Have you watched the Tom Hanks movie, *Cast Away*? The character he portrayed was a busy head. He did not even have enough time to have a meaningful conversation with his fiancee. As destiny goes, his plane crashed and he was stranded on an island all by himself and had nobody to talk to. As a result, he created an imaginary person from a volleyball, Wilson, and started having conversations and even arguments with him. More often than not, we don't treasure something until we lose it.

Music and sound is magical

Wellness trends come and go, but sound healing isn't one of them. It has been around since ancient times. For example, in Greece, scholars used music to cure mental disorders. Sound is magical. It has the power to motivate people, but also to bring them down. It can turn people happy in minutes, but it can also put them in a melancholic and reminiscent state. In the ancient imperial Chinese court, there was an officer whose sole job and responsibility was to create music for harmony in the country. In fact, pop stars are worshiped like Gods in this day and age. This is why so many people want to be the next pop star in AMERICA GOT TALENT.

How does sound healing work?

If we go deep into the sub-atomic space, everything is vibration, which is sound. So, the whole of creation is in fact a giant symphony. Moreover, the human body is 75% water. Water is a great vibration conductor. Singing, humming, singing bowls, mantras or simply listening to music can entrance your being with that particular vibrational frequency, thus shifting energies in the body and mind.

Medically speaking, studies show that listening to music makes our brain release dopamine and oxytocin. These hormones make us feel happy and relaxed. This helps with learning new skills and increases creativity. It helps with stress, mood swings, sleep, and even blood pressure or digestive issues. Music helps babies and children quiet down.

Psychologically speaking, sound and music can play a big role in healing trauma, especially when it's challenging for someone to recollect a space-time before the traumatic event happened. Hearing particular vibrations can trigger the memory of when we were in our mother's womb. Being in a mother's womb can be the safest and most secure space-time for a very traumatized person.

What is the most powerful sound healing tool?

We have three times more direct neural connections between the ears and the brain than we do between the eyes and the mighty muscle. We never stop hearing, not even when we sleep. The whole body connects with the ears, the throat is actually in sync with the inner ear.

When we are anxious, even as children, we hum, sing or pray. Have you ever been on a flight that you thought was about to crash? If so, you would probably pray to GOD or whoever or whatever right? One of the reasons we do this is because we can hear our own voice from the inside that charges our nerves and this vibration quiets our inner turmoil. There are many instruments that we can use to practice sound or music healing, but the most powerful one will always be our own voice. We all have the power to heal ourselves.

Tools in sound healing

Every culture and religion has prayers from Christian, to Muslims, Buddhists or whatever religion you can think of. In fact, praying is listening to your own voice, a form of sound healing. Some devoted people go to church, temple or synagogue regularly. This gives them a sense of wanting to give back and makes them feel part of something bigger. Some prefer to pray at home alone regularly.

Many people prefer tools like sound bowls, gongs, bells, musical instruments, or a guru's mantra chanting recording. They help to calm the mind by making the brain entranced and focused on the sound. These tools help quiet our "monkey mind". It allows us to connect with our spiritual ear, thus helping "THE SILENCE" speak.

When and where to use sound healing?

In the end, we're left with asking ourselves: when is the best time to practice sound healing? Should we first find peace? Should we invest in gadgets or special tools? Should we do it alone or as part of a group? The answer is "JUST DO IT"

As a rule of thumb, You should practice it when You don't have the time and You don't feel like yourself. It seems contradictory, but it is the truth. You will never have the time if You don't make the time. You don't need fancy equipment. You only need You.

You don't need to travel anywhere, but You do have to travel inward. You can imagine You are on top of a mountain listening to Mother Nature from the comfort of Your home or the intimacy of the hotel. You can do it in the bathroom or bedroom, with friends, as a group activity. You decide.

The importance of a "white wall" for beginners

Kash, the author, says: "Someone says: If it fails, It is better to fail quickly, early and safely. I once went to a meditation camp. The teacher asked us rookie meditation practitioners to sit cross-legged on the floor, in front of a white wall. They said that this is to avoid distractions, bra bra bra. We were in our pajamas or undies, as it was a hot room with no AC. Actually, it was very challenging, even for 10 minutes. You can try to allow 10 minutes to pass by watching a wall, not doing anything but clearing your mind and breathing, in a hot room with no AC. Retrospectively, it was a waste of time and money. Instead, I should have just watched a YouTube video and did it myself at home to see if I liked it or not before committing $600 USD and a 3-day long weekend."

We meditate to clear our minds. Ideally, it should be an effortless effort. We don't push thoughts away, as thoughts will always be there. We can use the metaphor of sitting by the window inside a room next to a street with beautiful scenery. Thoughts are like the traffic. We have little control over the traffic,yet we don't have to be distracted by the cars nor chase them. We acknowledge them, relax, and keep enjoying the beautiful scenery.

There is a difference between fighting our inner dragon and saluting the dragon with bait, such as mantra, music, sound or prayer. This is the first step to evolution, which is being flexible and skillful. As humans, we can make the choice of becoming a better version of ourselves with whatever tools that are available. We can set ourselves up for greatness and equip ourselves with whatever tools fit the circumstance. Let's do some sound healing?

Now use your most vibrant creative juice to write a script for yourself and your partner of how you can balance your own vibration and your partner's. Spend at least 10 minutes and let your imagination go wild. Then, go to the suggested exercises scripts chapter to see what we have for you.

Now. Scribble with your hands or your mind's eye. Enjoy!

8. Grow Mindfulness With Your Partner's Breath

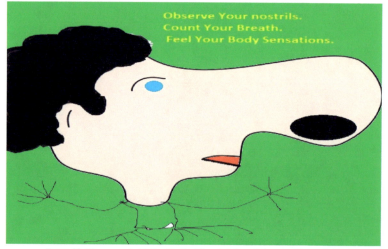

Figure 10. We come onto Mother Earth with an inhale and depart with an exhale

My best non-human friend, Dustin The Bull Dog, barks: "Breathe is my life and smell is my guide."

We come to earth with an inhalation and depart with an exhalation. In many cultures, spirit and breath are synonyms. Breath is the key to a relaxed mind with laser sharp focus. It can help us to stop, calm, rest and heal. Almost all creatures need to breathe or else death is certain. Yet, we seldom take the time to learn to do it right. Most of us humans do not actualize the full benefits of what our breath process can bring us. Although we have developed many tools we need as an evolved species, we seldom take a deep look at our own body, which is the most marvelous machine tool of the universe.

When we think about the sense of smell and the breath, we don't always connect the dots. These two processes are instilled in us since birth. Breathing in our mother's smell connects us to our mother from the first minutes of life, while smelling nasty odors keeps us away from harm. A newborn's sight is developing as he or she experiences the world, but it can count on it's sense of smell from the start. The nose helps us differentiate between our mothers and other people; it is an unconscious survival behavior to reach for our mother. The sense of smell keeps us close to our mothers and makes us fidget when we don't smell her close. Scientists say that breathing plays a big role in choosing our partners or friends, too.

Smell is tied to the brain's limbic system, the one responsible for our feelings of elated uplifting emotions or traumatic depressing experiences. We can "smell memories". Have you ever had the experience of smelling your favorite childhood food, and instantly your mind travels back to your childhood home where your mother made that food? The nose's olfactory receptor neurons, which we can find behind our sinuses, are the only receptor neurons able to live exposed to air. These neurons package the message of smell that will be delivered to the piriform cortex, the inside neurons that identify the smell. Because its position is so close to the hippocampus and the amygdala, it plays a big role in unconscious memory retention.

Do we know our own breathing process?

Have you ever caught your breath after intense exercise? Perhaps it is the only time you pay attention to this life and death process. It seems simple. In and out, in and out is all it takes. However, if you look deeper,it is a very complicated process. If I ask you, how does your breath relate to your body and mind? Perhaps you will answer,"I pant heavily during sex and strenuous exercises ", "I take a deep inhale and hold when I lift something very heavy or when I need to push while taking a shit". When you go through heightened states of mind, your heart rhythm elevates. At the same time, your breathing also quickens. It is because your nerves and many of your life-sustaining organs demand more energy. Have you noticed when you inhale, you elongate your spine a little bit? Your lungs expand like an accordion to bring in new oxygen to cells. You inhale before flexing the body and you exhale to contract the diaphragm. When you take the time to let the air in, you also lengthen muscles and expand them like a balloon. After all, honestly, do you experientially know your breathing and feel this intricate process up from every muscle, tendon, diaphragm movement, and sensation the nerves generate? Breathing is a profound process and most of us only know the tip of the iceberg. Gautama, the Buddha, says that it is possible to make this unconscious process conscious at the cellular and atomic level.

Breathing and Performance

Deep rhythmic breathing helps cleanse the body, as well as to carry nutrients to help us recover better and faster. Professional athletes have used special oxygen therapy to speed up their recovery. Breathing properly is critical when you want to move your body efficiently and effectively. Your Yoga instructor might have told you "it's all in the breath". Breathing can be the new exercises that can help you become the best version of yourself. Many professional athletes practice breathing to increase performance, reduce inflammation and joint stiffness, but also as a motivator to keep going strong. In fact, Stig Severin, four-time world freediving champion and holder of multiple Guinness World Records, created Breatheology to do just that. There isn't only one way to breathe right, but there sure is one that is perfect for you. We, the authors, encourage you to explore and learn more about breatheology as we did, as we have benefited much from this teaching. For regular folks, these deep breathing techniques help reboot the body when we aren't feeling our best. For example, during a cold or allergies, it helps to perform deep breathing as much as possible. More importantly, deep breathing helps to refresh our minds, especially during extended periods of intense focus. Why do you yawn? Because our body craves for fresh air. If you need more energy now, just take a big breath of fresh air NOW and imagine all your cells are smiling at you as they LOVE fresh oxygen. Do this again and again until you feel fresh and energized.

Breathing and Our Unconscious Body Processes.

If breathing stops, our life stops. Almost all of our life processes are unconscious. Deep rhythmic breathing releases tension, anxieties, and melancholy. It increases our creativity and decreases our addictive behaviors. It aids the immune system. It is beneficial for people with hypertension or asthma to practice deep breathing regularly. In fact, breathing helps regulate our body temperature and immune system. Wim-Hoff has demonstrated that with his special breathing protocol, he and his students can sustain exposure to freezing cold temperatures with minimal clothing or no clothing for extended periods. Also, during another experiment, he and his students demonstrated that they can control their immune systems with this special breathing protocol. Again, we, the authors, encourage you to explore and learn more about the Wim-Hof Method, as we have benefited much from this teaching.

When to practice breathing exercises?

Everybody, anywhere, can do deep rhythmic breathing. In the car while stuck in traffic, on the airplane taking off, in the kitchen when everybody is fussing around, and even at work. Deep rhythmic breathing can help calm your nerves in any stressful situation, such as a school exam or a job interview, when you are booked and feel anxiety while waiting to get your mugshot taken, when you are about to get your nipples, clitoris or penis glans pierced. Deep rhythmic breathing helps us with these kinds of overwhelming scenarios that can bring us into hysteria. When we are in a situation where we don't know what to say or how to react, it's best to stop, take a few deep breaths and get ourselves centered. If we find ourselves in the freeze mode of significant stress, we should continue with this deep breathing and count our breaths like one, two, three... until we are calm and centered. Army forces do it, athletes do it, yogis do it and YOU CAN DO IT TOO. Strong feelings, such as anger and lust, can take over even the calmest of spirits, but the breath is always the right antidote. Take your time, don't react and practice deep breathing, in and out, in and out.

Breathing can be used a painkiller

Deep Breathing helps to reduce many symptoms. Deep Breathing consciously helps mothers bring new souls into the world faster, with ease, and while feeling more energized. If you ever witness a natural childbirth, the mother is always asked to breathe deeply. A natural childbirth is the most intense physical pain a human can experience, according to scientists. For people who have not yet experienced giving birth, perhaps imagine a spiky pineapple coming out of your butt hole. If breathing can help with this pain, then the process of breathing can be the most powerful painkiller living in ourselves. You can do this experiment by having someone pinch your sensitive area forcefully. Ask your partner to pinch your inner upper thigh before and after the WIM-HOFF Breathing method and see if there is any difference.

The authors tried this experiment. It feels less painful after doing the WIM-HOFF Breathing method. In a nutshell, the WIM-HOFF breathing is to inhale quickly and deeply through the mouth or nose, which the authors prefer, and then to exhale quickly using the mouth without any force. Just relax with dropping jaws and let the breath go out by itself. Do this breathing protocol until one feels the tingling sensations all over your body and then ask your partner to pinch your sensitive area of your choice. You should feel less pain, hopefully.

Breathing, Mindfulness and Meditation

Breathing properly is the first step in meditation. Mediation represents different things for different people. Some chant mantras, others meditate with their eyes open gazing at something. Some even say whatever they see, hear, smell, touch, or taste can be a form of meditation. In fact, this is what Gautama the Buddha says is the eventual goal of every meditator. One is meditating with mindfulness every moment 24 / 7, even while the body is in deep sleep.

Many traditions use breathing as a tool for mediation. This meditation involves putting our awareness on the breathing process. It means focusing on the body sensations, emotions and thoughts induced by the breathing process. For example, we scan every inch of our body, from head to toe during our inhale and exhale. In the beginning, we might need some guidance to start till it becomes a habit in our being. Breathing meditation helps improve body image and studies show that, in time, it has the ability to improve the brain, which means you have evolved into an upgraded version of yourself.

In many Hatha yoga schools, one starts with asanas, poses that move our body with rhythmic breathing. Then there is pranayama, the breathing technique. One of the goals of pranayama is to have a balanced breath. However, what is a balanced breath? One of the criteria of a balanced breath is to have the flow of left and right nostrils equal.

Shiva Swarodaya is an ancient Sanskrit text about Swara yoga, which means the yoga for analysis of breath and practicing of breath control. In Swara yoga, the left nostril is tied to the Lunar Breath and the right with the Solar breath. It's a known fact that our bodies are not completely balanced most of the time. Same with our breathing, we always have one nostril that is more open and allows the breath to flow better.

Nadis Sodana, a known pranayama practice, is the right and left alternate nostril breathing, in order to balance the breath. This is a way to calm the nervous system and cleanse the body by balancing the left and right nostril's breath flow. According to Ayurveda, it can cure headaches and many nerve-related symptoms. Modern research shows that our brain becomes more balanced when we are balancing the two brain hemispheres by balancing the Yin (Lunar Breath. Left Nostril) and Yang (Solar Breath. Right Nostril) breathe with pranayama, such as Nadi Shodhana. Hardcore yogis take it one step further and use a stick to balance the breath. In fact, you can buy this stick online. It is called Yoga danda stick. Depending on which of the nostrils is dominant, let's say the right is, this means the right needs to be less dominant. Yogi puts a stick in the right armpit and presses against it. This will help to open the left nostril and increase its flow and reduce the flow of the right nostril, hence balancing the breath.

Sense of Smell and Instincts

Depending on the human diet and hormones, people emit specific scents. In fact every person's scent is unique. A police dog can pinpoint a specific person just by sniffing his or her clothing. Recent research shows that when women are fertile, they will look for a specific odor in their partners, usually, one whose genetics are different to their own. Women who are not fertile, or are taking contraceptives, will actually look for a completely different scent. These facts are based on recent studies done on small groups. The results seem obvious and it's fascinating to consider that smell does affect us socially and sexually.

Isn't smell the most powerful human sense? Have you ever been to a very dirty, foul smell restroom such as an overflowing portable toilet at a festival? What would you do? Hold your breath, finish the business as quickly as possible and GET OUT as if life depends on it? A mind-blowing experiment for you: imagine smelling other people's feces, vomit or spoiled cheese while eating your most favorite food at the same time. If it passes your imagination, would you dare to do it as well? I bet you cannot convince yourself to open your mouth at that moment. Perhaps you can manage by NOT breathing, if you are famished. If you are not famished, I bet you would NOT chew and just have the food swallowed. Kash had that experience at a party. Yet, there might be some humans who can achieve this feat of wonder. We, the authors, would bow down and salute or have compassion for you if you could breathe and fully embrace foul-smelling shit while eating your favorite food.

If you do this experiment for real, please make a video. Please share with us. If you post it on social media, this video might become viral, but your account may get banned. So be cautious of the consequences.

Aromatherapy

Everything is dual. A foul smell can kill us and a good smell can heal us. This takes us to aromatherapy, which we can use to both relax our bodies and minds, but also to conjure memories in a safe and controlled environment to heal. Some businesses use smell as a marketing tool, like baking bread in a house that is on the market or spraying flowery scents in SPAs to help get us in the right mindset to be able to relax.

Studies show that the smell of coffee makes people focus on time, while lavender calms the nervous system and lemon oil has the ability to make us productive for longer periods. Smell matters, and it has many powers, both curative and unappealing ones.

We live in a sensory world. Do you know that our ears connect with the nose and the eyes connect with each other? Try crying like no tomorrow without having any liquid running out from your nose. Or try putting on ear plugs, then take a deep inhale, and then close your nostrils and mouth and exhale. All these sense organs work as a team to paint a picture of our surroundings for our brain, which is inside the most secret and secure dark enclosure of our body. So, even though our nose matters a lot, the eyes count even more when it comes to "feeling it out". We often smell something before the aroma reaches our nostrils, if our eyes see it, our eyes send the message to the brain much faster.

For example, imagine a brand of ice cream that looks like feces, yet it tastes and smells the best in the world. We, the authors, have not yet found this brand. We are sure nobody will buy this shit-looking ice cream and that the company who made it is already bankrupt.

Perfume

Perfume making is an art. It takes a special nose and a chemistry diploma to successfully mix fragrance notes. A perfume depends on the construction of the top, middle and base notes, but also on the wearer– because the perfume mixes with the skin's natural oils, and the one doing the smelling. One perfume can be wonderful on one's skin and awful on another skin type because of the different pH levels of each person.

All in all, olfaction is an intriguing subject for many specialists. This is because of its ability to process many sensors and pass them through a complex system that can affect us emotionally, cognitively, and even socially. The sense of smell can calm nerves or put us in lucidity, imagine the smell of cannabis and the smell of lemon. The sense of smell also has a major influence on how we perceive people. Imagine the very foul smell of bad breath from a very sexy mate during a blind date. This can make a lusty human retreat to the comfort of his or her home immediately.

There are perfumes and fragrances infused with human pheromones on the market. It claims that these products can trigger the opposite sex's unconscious sexual desires. It says that male Cecropia moths can detect the female moth in heat many hundred miles away by her pheromone. It then flies many hundred miles away to copulate and reproduce with her.

We, the authors, have never tried these human-pheromone-infused products. We, the authors, suppose that if a moth's pheromones work, then human pheromones should work too? However, the influence is probably very subtle and unconscious. similar to the woman's smell researchers have described earlier in the chapter. We humans most often suppress our innate instincts with social boundaries, protocols and expected behaviors. This is fortunate and unfortunate.

MINDFULNESS MEDITATION

Anapana means observation of Breath. Breath is a process that accompanies us in every moment. We take our first inhale breath when our body comes out of our mother's womb. We take our last exhale breath when our body has expired. We rarely pay much attention to this process. Gautama the Buddha taught his followers Anapana as the primary form of meditation. It is documented in Satipatthana Sutta, Ānāpānasati Sutta and Visuddhimagga. It is the main meditation for mindfulness in Theravada, Tiantai and Zen Buddhism.

From the internet: The meaning of mindfulness:

- The quality or state of being conscious or aware of something.

- A mental state achieved by focusing one's awareness on the present moment, while calmly acknowledging and accepting one's feelings, thoughts, and bodily sensations, used as a therapeutic technique.

As we choose to be the observer and use our thoughts, emotions and sensations as objects of observation, we give ourselves the opportunity to step out of being the character of our game. This is the first step of self-reflection and self-regulation. This is the first step of transformation and making fundamental changes. Some claim that only humans have this ability. In Anaprana, we use our breath as an object of observation. In mindfulness practice, we extend the object to our bodily sensations, emotions and thoughts. The most important aspect of the practice is to know and act as if we are only the observer. We are NOT the doer. We are NOT the participants. We just sit back, relax and enjoy the show. As one recalls from the previous chapter, the observed always get affected by the observer and the process of observation. As a result, our emotions, thoughts, bodily sensations and breath change during the process of observation. Most of the time, our emotions, thoughts, bodily sensations and breath tend to quiet down during the process of observation.

Moorea, the Author says: "I participated in a meditation camp in the Theravada tradition. They taught Anapana and mindfulness meditation there. When I first started the Anapana meditation and mindfulness meditation, I had many instances of strong memories and negative emotions of being abused as a child. I had the urge to get up and just leave the camp. However, my inner voice told me just to relax, observe and stay. I did, and eventually these emotions and memories passed. I talked to my guide and she said I was doing the right thing. The trick is to wait it out and have it pass away, just like watching a storm. As my practice continued, I learned more and more to just be the observer. Eventually, these emotions and memories lost their impact on me. It is not like I don't have those memories and emotions, but I empowered myself with tools to handle them and minimize the impact they have on me."

Mindfulness Meditation

It says that during a period, LA Lakers and Chicago Bulls dominated and won many championships, and their head coach, Phil Jackson, claims to have used mindfulness meditation as a performance-enhancing tool for his teams. As research indicates, even 10 minutes every day of mindfulness meditation can set us up for success. What is mindfulness? Many masters say it's being aware. So, it requires an observer, an object being observed and the process of observation. Breath and body sensations are considered the easiest and safest to observe. For regular folks, emotions and thoughts can be too abstract to observe. Most often than not, we also get lost in observing our emotions and thoughts, especially those associated with past experiences that had a deep impact on us, such as trauma and abusive experiences. From the experience of past meditators and recent research, it's shown that there is always a signal manifested in our nervous system as a bodily sensation, whenever an emotion or thought arises. As a result, we can always use our bodily sensations to observe our emotions and thoughts indirectly.

Moreover, our memory is also embedded in our cells as discussed previously in the event of an organ receiver in a transplant operation. Again, from the previous chapter, we discussed the possibilities that we can reprogram our being with positive emotions and thoughts. With the same token, by observing the corresponding body part with a neutral and relaxed attitude, we are resetting our cells at the atomic level. We can only get new fresh water into our cup when it's clean and empty. Mindfulness Meditation can mean a holiday for our mind and body. We don't even have to clear our minds completely. We can let thoughts come and go, just like watching a show. Similarly, we just observe all our sensory inputs and bodily sensations and let them be, no matter if they are pleasant, unpleasant or neutral. We just let it be, relax and be in the moment of HERE and NOW. We need to realize that every moment is a completely new moment. We only live in the HERE and NOW,

Now use your most vibrant creative juice to write a script for yourself and your partner of how you can up level your own mindfulness and your partner's. Spend at least 10 minutes and let your imagination go wild. Then, go to the suggested exercises scripts chapter to see what we have for you.

Now. Scribble with your hands or your mind's eye. Enjoy!

9. Grow Intimacy With Your Partner's Hands and Fingers

Figure 11. Its a relationship milestone when we held hands during our middle school summer camp

Above Image for Tattoo Idea for Couple Tattoo Number One.

The hands are one of the humblest parts of our being. Humans are set apart from other creatures because of our brain and our hands. In many cultures, two people wanted to show they have a genuine connection, they usually hold hands with fingers intertwined or not. We can express ourselves so much just by using our hands. As the most frequently used body parts, they are susceptible to many injuries, from cuts and burns to more serious issues, like arthritis. Many people can work long hours with their hands, whether it is serving the table or writing at a computer. Yet, they feel they have weak hands when practicing yoga, or rock climbing. Why is that? Perhaps, we need to show more attention, care and love our hands deserve.

We need to know about our hands.

The hand, although fragile at first glance, is very complex. It allows us to do powerful things, like fight with it, but also delicate things, like fix watches, make precious jewelry and comfort meals, play a musical instrument or paint a

The hands are one of the humblest parts of our being. Humans are set apart from other creatures because of our brain and our hands. In many cultures, if two people want to show they have a genuine connection, they usually hold hands, with fingers intertwined or not. We can express ourselves so much just by using our hands. As the most frequently used body parts, they are susceptible to many injuries, from cuts and burns to more serious issues, like arthritis. Many people can work long hours with their hands, whether it is serving a table or writing at a computer. Yet, they feel they have weak hands when practicing yoga, or rock climbing. Why is that? Perhaps, we need to show our hands the attention, care and love they deserve.

We need to know more about our hands.

The Muscle system located in the forearm is one of the most sophisticated. It controls the hand movements. The flexible wrist, long tendons and finger bones are so complicated that scientists cannot fully replicate the human hand in a robot. The hands have a lot of nerves and nerve endings. The skin plays a big role in protecting them, and it has sensors to tell if something is smooth, spikey, wet, dry, hot, or cold. Again, we cannot fully replicate such a protective layer. Skin-like protective armor with sensors would be a must for super soldiers.

The hands use a lot of brain power because they have a lot of nerves and nerve endings. They send signals to the spinal cord. The spinal cord carries these signals along and sends them to the thalamus and the thalamus carries these signals eventually to the primary sensory cortex. The high demand of computational power of the hands is best represented by the cortical homunculus. This is a distorted representation of the body, based on the sensory homunculus and motor homunculus. They are brain maps dedicated to sensory and motor messages coming from different parts of the body. Doctor Wilder Penfield is one of the first scientists to discover this. His "grotesque creature" has oversized hands, because of the brainpower they need, compared to the torso and arms, which are quite small.

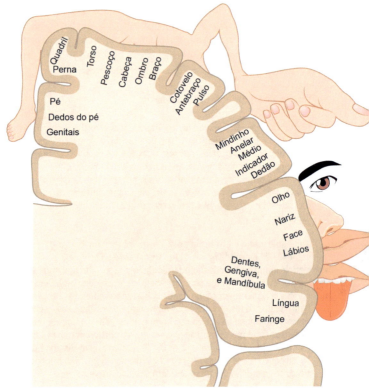

Figure 12. Cortical Homunculus.

Everyone talks with their hands.

The hands are some of the recipients that get to connect us to our wishes. They make it possible for us to eat, embrace, caress, carry, wash and pray to name but a few. Hands also say a lot about us and our feelings. When we're confident, we tend to keep them open. When we're shy, sad, or angry, we usually carry them close to our bodies, wrapped or even in clenched fists. When we're anxious, we have sweaty and sticky hands, a slight tremble, or we crack our fingers.

We can talk using our hands too. Besides sign language, we also use our hands for other messages. We put one finger out to point to something or draw attention and the thumbs up for "OK", we cross fingers for good luck, we put two fingers up as a peace sign or as "rock on", we put all our fingers up to answer in class, we make a fist to show the power and we put both our hands together to pray or to say "namaste" – the light in me bows to the light in you. The hands are marvelous explainers of our insides.

The best public speakers know that for the public to receive their message well, they have to use hand gestures that carry their ideas and influence people. We use hands to talk from early toddlerhood when we sing child songs, test new ingredients, or as comfort during teething periods.

Scientists have discovered that blind people talk to other blind people with their hands too. We use gestures to access ideas faster, to convey them better, and for the recipient to also remember our ideas for long periods of time. There are many games we played growing up that use the hands, like mime games. Who hasn't used the hands to show "small", "big" or even shapes like "square" or "heart"?

One of the most useful things we do with our hands is cross-cultural. When we travel and don't know how to say certain words in our native tongue, we understand each other through the language of our hands, which is universal. Of course when we travel, it's best to learn whether certain hand gestures mean something different in specific countries. For example, putting up the peace sign or the crossed fingers for good luck might mean you're giving the FRUK-finger to somebody from the UK or Vietnam.

Hand Reflexology

Hand reflexology is a classic technique to heal the body. There are many pressure points that connect specific areas of the human vessel. By applying the right force, we can de-stress our muscles and organs to relieve pain and even heal.

The father of reflexology in America is doctor William Fitzgerald. He introduced these exercises to the continent in 1915, but many practitioners believe reflexology started in China or Egypt. This technique is usually practiced by a specialist, especially for more serious issues, but also can be practiced by ourselves to ourselves, or to each other.

When we're stressed or have a headache, we use our hands to press specific points on our face to get relief. There are many benefits to reflexology, but this touch therapy should not be used as a cure-all type of technique, but as an alternative treatment to complement others.

The biggest advantage of reflexology compared to acupuncture, for example, is that it is safe for everybody to use by themselves. There is no equipment necessary. It is believed that if a person gives somebody else a massage, the one giving will also receive part of the energy from the person he or she is giving the massage to. So, it is important to cleanse your energy by taking a shower or burning sage over yourselves after giving a massage, especially when you don't know that person very well.

When to practice reflexology?

Any time is a good time to practice hand reflexology. Imagine during a date, your potential mate offers you a hand and foot reflexology session for 20 minutes. After that, he or she asks you how you feel, and you go, "it feels wonderful." Fortunately and unfortunately, your date might go, "thanks for letting me give you a massage,now $50 USD please. Just joking" We, the authors, suggest that you offer a hand reflexology to your partner or potential partner for free. GENUINE LOVE and CONNECTION is PRICELESS. Someone says: "The most important thing in life is Freedom and it's free. For example: Air, Water, Sunshine, Love is free." Do you agree?

Reflexology can be done safely for over 150 conditions, but there are also some conditions which are best to avoid using this treatment on to cure. For example, reflexology isn't recommended in the last months of pregnancy, for serious injuries like fractures, or during periods of inflammation. It's also best to avoid putting pressure on specific points if you're taking medication that thins the blood or if you have skin irritations. So, we advise you and your partner to start exploring each other's hands and feet by giving gentle massages. "JUST DO IT." If that particular hand or foot region is sensitive or painful when receiving a massage, that reflexology zone probably needs more love from you. So be gentle.

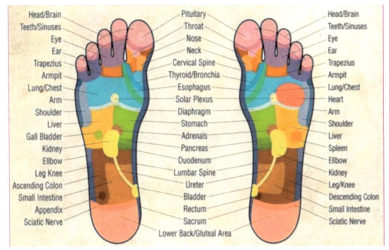

Figure 13. Sole Foot Reflex Zones

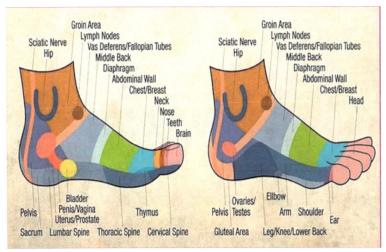

Figure 14. Side Foot Reflex Zones

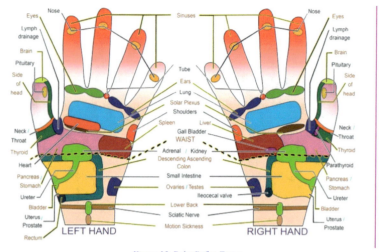

Figure 15. Palm Reflex Zones

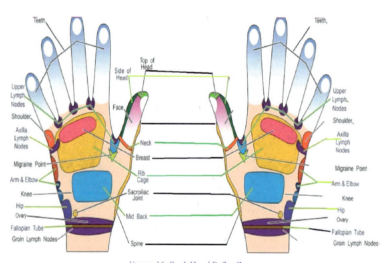

Figure 16. Back Hand Reflex Zones

Hand Mudra

We can use hand signals to communicate with another human who speaks a different language. Can we do the same with beings who inhabit dimensions beyond our own? Can the device of transmission be our own body parts such as hands and fingers? Can the messages be delivered in the form of body sensations, sounds, images and insights that are often ignored by our conscious mind? Recall in an earlier chapter that our bodies can communicate to us and predict future events. Do you notice when we communicate, most of the time it is non-verbal? Remember when you were in a concert and felt so high that you fist pumped and rocked out with the songs before you ever said a word to your pal next to you?

In the yoga culture, there are well-known hand mudras that are practiced for communication to our higher-self, the aspect of ourselves that is fully evolved and is beyond space and time. Imagine if the NOW you time and space traveled to the 6-year-old you and gave him or her guidance. Life is a continuum and there is a future version of you that is fully evolved and all knowing, like a "GOD or GODDESS". This higher-self can give you guidance here and now. Mudras can help you to communicate with this higher-self for guidance on specific topics.

The selection of mudras discussed here are based on the authors' personal experience. We, the authors, feel that these mudras help give us insights. They help bring us back to balance and have more bliss during meditation and pranayama practice. It is a non-verbal communication by means of the hands and fingers. It can do the same for you!

Now use your most vibrant creative juice to write a script for yourself and your partner of how you can up level your own life force and your partner's using your hands. Spend at least 10 minutes and let your imagination go wild. Then, go to the suggested exercises scripts chapter to see what we have for you. Enjoy!

Example of Hand Mudras

According to yogic tradition, each of our five fingers are connected to a specific element.
Thumb connects to the space element. Index finger connects to the air element. Middle finger connects to the fire element. Ring finger connects to the water element. Little finger connects to the earth element. If you are math-minded, then you can see that there are many possible configurations for the fingers to make up the mudras. However, because of modern human bodies becoming increasingly acidified and NOT flexible due to unnatural living, many of those configurations are NOT available. If you have access to very young humans around 1-3 years old, you can try to make Mudras with them and can make a good game out of it.

Gyan Mudra or Knowledge Mudra

This is likely the most recognizable. It resembles the OK sign. Gyan mudra helps us focus with a relaxed attitude. This is a wonderful mudra to utilize when we intend to meditate and download information from the universe.

This mudra is performed by contacting the tip of the index finger (Air) to the tip of the thumb (space); hence making a circular hole. At the same time, stretch the other three fingers out and make them straight.

Buddhi Mudra or Clarity Mudra

This mudra helps us to clear our minds. It heightens our intuition, especially when we need that extra boost to comprehend a message, such as a dream or a vision from our unconscious self.

This mudra is performed by contacting the tip of the thumb to the tip of the pinky finger, while stretching out the other three fingers straight. Note that the pinky finger connects to the earth element, which is dominated by our stomach. Have you ever felt that funny feeling in your stomach during an insightful moment?

Shunya Mudra or Space Mudra

This mudra improves the space element by activating the fire element with the middle finger. As a result, it also helps to increase our alertness, and sensitivity. It helps to purify our junk emotions and garbage thoughts which are more often than NOT, embedded in our bodily junk. You can think of it as an energetic colonic.

This mudra is performed by touching the tip of the middle finger to the thumb tip, while keeping the other three fingers stretched out straight and relaxed.

Prana Mudra or Sword Mudra

Sword Mudra or Prana Mudra helps to focus your prana. Taoist priests and Reiki masters use this mudra to empower the symbol during enchantment and healing rituals.

This mudra is performed by touching the tip of the thumb with the ring and little fingers, while keeping the other two fingers straight.

Dhyana Mudra or Meditation Mudra

The Dhyana mudra is used over many mindfulness traditions. The Gautama Buddha is frequently pictured doing this mudra. This mudra helps to bring you into a more profound, relaxed focus, which is the key for meditation. This mudra can also help bring you quietness and inward harmony.

This mudra is performed with your palms facing upward, right hand laying on top of your left palm with the tips of the thumb touching, making a circle, which signifies endless perfection.

Surya Mudra or Sun Mudra

The Surya mudra helps to increase the sun-powered fire element in the body. It improves digestion and metabolism. It helps avert colds, especially when practiced with heating pranayama such as Bhastrika.

Perform this mudra by twisting your ring finger so that the ring finger's second knuckle is touching the base of the thumb and the tip of your thumb contacts the ring finger's first knuckle. At the same time stretch your other three fingers straight without straining the hand.

Gyan Mudra

Buddhi Mudra

Shunya Mudra

Prana Mudra

Dhyana Mudra

Now use your most vibrant creative juice to write a script for yourself and your partner of how you can up level your own life force and your partner's using your hands and fingers. Spend at least 10 minutes and let your imagination go wild. Then, go to the suggested exercises scripts chapter to see what we have for you.

Now. Scribble with your hands or your mind's eye. Enjoy!

Figure 23. My teacher says you can make someone fall in love with you by sucking the nipples, rubbing the inner thighs or massaging the feet.

Picture Above:Couples' Tattoo Idea Number Two.

Have you ever got a tiny splinter in the bottom of your feet? It's so tiny that you cannot imagine how it is possible that it can create so much pain and suffering to the point where your first priority in life at that moment is to get rid of that tiny little splinter. In fact the human toes, feet and legs are very special, so are we compared to the rest of the creation.

The human legs and feet are special, not because we think of ourselves as superior beings, but because we are using them differently. Some animals here and there stand on their feet, but we are the only creature that walks and runs on just two legs. Feet carry us everywhere, they help us climb, dance, and run marathons, but they also connect us to Earth.

When we aren't feeling our best, it's important to take a moment to reach inside and reconnect. The feet are a powerful source of energy, but also love and lust. The lower part of the body is the most used and in this fast-forward life, we hardly take the time to give them undivided attention. We usually do it when pain arises, but we have to learn to bring awareness to them more often.

We need to know more about our feet.

We have two legs, two feet, and ten toes, five for each of the lower parts. The feet take up a quarter of our body's bones, more precisely, 52 of them. Paying attention to this area is very important, especially with old age. The big and little toes help us with balance, and if your toes are essential, they deserve some attention.

After the age of 25, our heart starts beating slower and slower and so our organs' circulation starts to deteriorate. Collagen levels drop and this has a major impact over our elasticity. Muscles get weaker, the skin gets flabby, cartilage loses its density. Without any remedies, our legs and feet get weaker and weaker. With aging, our feet and legs become more susceptible to injuries or arthritis, especially when we don't take good care of them. However, there are natural ways to strengthen our legs and feet.

We need optimal alignment and proper weight distribution to walk this Earth for as long as we can. Stretching, Earthing, and acupuncture are natural ways to connect to the universal energy and to ourselves.
One last thing before we dive deeper into different practices,yogis are the first sources of inspiration who really draw attention to the feet. They always preach about the importance of our postures. We have to spread the toes wide when walking or standing and we have to wear comfortable shoes that let our feet breathe and connect with the floor.

They also remind us to sit up evenly on both feet, tuck our pelvis and suck in our bellies for full support of our bodies. A regular check-in to connect and position goes a long way. Don't worry if it doesn't come easy in the beginning, you are undoing many years of physical and psychological tension.

What do our feet signify?

To continue the journey into Yoga and the feet veneration, many students kiss the feet of their teachers. The feet are a symbol of teachings that have been passed on through each generation and they are the foundation of the temple. Just like a building's structure, if the base is not balanced, it will not offer the right support. If you don't know what to think about your feet, let's analyze your steps. Walk to the closest pair of shoes, it's best if it is a pair of winter boots, and check the sole. Everybody has a personalized walk and the sole wears out differently based on how you walk.

Do you walk inside of your foot or outside? Do you put pressure on the toes or on the heel? Which one of your legs is more dominant? Which one carries more weight? Your shoes and your footprints say a lot about how you use and treat your feet.

You might think that a building is static, that once you set the pillars, it is done. But that's not the case. Everything is connected to Mother Earth, who is always moving. Most buildings will get damaged during a severe earthquake. Imagine if a building's pillars are flexible like your feet and can flow with mother earth's movement. Our body is designed and created like so, to flow with mother earth. Flexible and agile legs and feet are necessary.

The first stand is to learn how to stand and carry yourself better. Yoga asana also comes to the rescue with the pose Tadasana or Mountain Pose. Learn the foundations of this one along with the Samastithi, the Equal Standing pose, to connect to the ground and also the sky. We, the authors, suggest you watch a video of standing pose from the Iyengar Yoga tradition or better yet, attend an Iyengar Yoga Certified teacher class. The Iyengar method emphasizes proper alignments which is critical to yoga asana practice especially for beginners who are not flexible or out of shape.

What are the benefits of Earthing?

Modern footwear limits blood flow. It crams the bones one next to the other, which results in clenched muscles and a tense body. In very ancient days, people used to walk barefoot and on uneven surfaces, which kept their feet flexible and adaptable. Today's environmental patterns– sitting at a desk and walking on heels– brings a lot of tension to our feet.

Walking around barefoot, or Earthing, is a natural and simple therapy available to everyone, everywhere, to connect our souls and bodies with the planet's energy. The concept is modern, but people have been doing it intuitively for ages. Walking on Mother Earth without shoes on helps access electrons that neutralize free radicals.

We can do Earthing alone, at any age, and it channels negative ions into the body. Few people think that their feet can be used as perfect conductors of Earth's energy. The foot has 250,000 sweat glands. The region of our feet has the highest sweat gland density which contain 600–700 sweat glands per square centimeter.

Grounding is a homemade remedy for many body afflictions, like inflammation or arthritis, but also more spiritual ones, like insomnia or depression. Everybody can tap into this energy by walking barefoot, but also by sitting outside, working the land, or even taking a nap on the grass. Before industrialization, people used to wear shoes with leather soles that were better at grounding than those made with plastic or rubber from today. However, being barefoot is the best. When we walk without shoes, our feet get the best massage out there, as we press specific points that connect to the rest of the body, like the liver, heart, lungs, brain, and the back muscles. It's instant energizing of the self, both inside and out.

How does Earth-ing work?

Have you noticed something is NOT right when you are being indoors most of the time during the week? Our bio-field and aura can only expand outdoors or in a structure built from natural materials such as wood, mud or straws. When our bio-field and aura expand, it gives us bliss and makes us happier. If you ever get locked up in jail or talk to someone who was in jail, one of the best treats is to get outdoors. The jail keeper knows, so they let the inmate get outdoors at least once or twice a week, at least in the jail in this country. Fresh air from the outdoors does the body wonders and so does walking bare foot or touching the earth with our hands.

Do you know that whenever we eat unnatural foods that are NOT intended for human consumption, our immune system will get triggered? In this scenario, our immune system wakes up our white blood cells. These little fighters release reactive oxygen molecules, or free radicals, to oxidize and eliminate what harms our bodies.

Free radicals have an electron imbalance and this makes them electrically charged. When they go looking for a free electron to neutralize, they can actually attach to a healthy cell. These healthy cells then become unhealthy. Mother earth is the largest capacitor and has an infinite amount of electrons that can help us to remove the free radicals and our oxidative stress. All we need to do is connect ourselves to earth and get recharged.

According to many natural doctors, oxidation stress, which is created by free radicals, is the root cause of most if not all chronic disease and illness. According to Dr. Rashid Buttar, there are seven major toxicities that contribute to oxidative stress in our body. They are "heavy metal toxicity, persistent organic pollutants (such as being exposed to harmful chemicals), opportunistic (such as bacteria, viruses, mycoplasma, yeast, etc.), energetics (such as microwaves, EMF, etc.), emotional psychological toxicity, food (not what we are eating but what we do to food such as homogenization, pasteurization, genetic modification, irradiation, etc.), and spiritual toxicity." The authors encourage the readers to look into Dr Rashid Buttar and his findings online.

Let's learn more about our First Chakra, which is deeply rooted in our legs, feet and toes. Let's remind ourselves from previous chapters...

Yoga is an art and science of the fusion of the physical and spiritual. It uses asanas and pranayama practice to activate energy vortex centers known as Chakras. l. These activated energy vortex centers help us to achieve elevated awareness. In the physical dimension, these seven energy vortex centers are nerve points. They connect with various organs and glands. The First Chakra is all about identity and survival on Earth as an individual. It is located at the base of the spine and gives us our survival instincts and sense of security and safety. The Root Chakra is connected to our feet via subtle nerves. In Indian and Tibetan tradition, our lust is channeled down towards our legs, feet and toes and vice versa. According to Indian and Tibetan traditional belief, if a person dies in a lower emotional state such as anger, the spirit will exit through the feet.

The First Chakra can be a gateway to disembodied souls, so when people die in India, their big toes are tied together to prevent the spirit from reentering the body. This is done especially during the rainy season, when cremation is sometimes postponed. The family of the deceased does it because they believe they will be haunted by a zombie otherwise.

The author's Indian friend had verified a counter example. A spirit possessed the dead body of his uncle because of the unmindfulness of his family. His uncle died in a remote village during the monsoon season in India. The cremation ceremony was delayed for 3 days because of the heavy monsoon rain. His family forgot to tie his dead uncle's big toes together. One night, the rain was not too heavy, but strangely enough there was plenty of thunder and lightning. In the middle of the night, his dead uncle sat straight up with bloody red eyes, murmuring. This freaky event lasts for over 10 minutes. The family members were literally scared shitless. They had no choice but to use gasoline to burn the dead body in the rain. Immediately after, the dead body was deactivated again. My friend said back then, smartphones were not popular, otherwise he would have made a video and made himself a TikTok sensation. Kash had tried making videos when he shit in his pants and can confirm that it's very challenging. We doubt he would be able to make the video even if he had a smartphone.

One last thing on the importance of bringing daily awareness to our feet: the feet and the pelvic floor are mirrors of each other. Elasticity and our posture determine the health of the First Chakra. In many traditional eastern cultures, it is custom to leave our shoes at the door. That is because it keeps our house clean. Second of all, because doing this creates a boundary by dividing the outside traffic and the intimacy of our home. A third note is that by walking barefoot at home, we are able to remember our feet and bring awareness to them.. It's important to free your feet to receive the Earth's energy at home. Shoes and concrete floors constrict mother earth's life force, which has the ability to give us a happy long life.

YOGIC POSTURE AS SACRED GEOMETRY CONFIGURATION

According to Yogic tradition, Mahamudra helps to balance the energy of Root Chakra. Most civilized humans ask their toddlers to control their bowel movement and introduce the concept of potty-training and the use of diapers. In fact, this can be the very first time a human experiences **CONDITIONAL LOVE and ACCEPTANCE.** The toddler has little control of the anal sphincter muscle. The authors do not know any pet and puppy caretaker that uses diapers on their pet, however, there is a double standard for humans. "Civilized" parents prefer the use of diapers and its convenience, rather than the discomfort of their offspring. It makes the toddler deviate from its natural state of bliss and love. As a result, it can be the moment that this toddler doubts God's complete unconditional love, which is supposed to be demonstrated by its parents. As a result, many humans have their Root Chakra compromised. Mahamudra is one of the best tools to address this. In fact, our human body is a blueprint of a cosmic antenna that can channel signals beyond space time. Yoga asanas postures resembling sacred geometry patterns can enhance this ability. The authors encourage the readers to learn more about this topic by learning more of Ibrahim Karim's Biogeometry.

Now use your most vibrant creative juice to write a script for yourself and your partner of how you tune up root chakra and your partner's. Spend at least 10 minutes and let your imagination go wild. Then, go to the suggested exercises scripts chapter to see what we have for you.

Now. Scribble with your hands or your mind's eye. Enjoy!

11. Suggested Exercises

Figure 24. The image: "Stare at me for 3 minutes."

This exercise helps you to manifest a partner if she or he has NOT shown up yet. If you are a couple, then it will bring your relationship onto the next level.

1	Now it is time to set aside 20-30 minutes to show some actual love to yourself. Do this activity with your partner or by yourself.
2	Make sure your phone is on silent to keep the distractions away .
3	Settle yourself in a comfortable space and sitting position.
4	Generate touch where your heart is on your chest.
5	Put a smile on your face and imagine your cells are smiling back at you.
6	Generate the feeling of appreciation, gratitude, care and compassion.
7	Take a deep breath and inhale for 4 seconds through the nose.
8	Hold the breath for about 1 second.
9	Exhale for 4 seconds with a relaxed face and jaw.
10	You can exhale through the mouth and make the sound like" HA" if you choose.
11	Pause for a second and feel the deep relaxation surrounding you.
12	Deep rhythmic breathing is really important. The fact is, it slows the brain waves,bringing them down to alpha and theta states.
13	You can continue this breathing pattern of 4:1:4:1 until you feel completely relaxed at each muscle of your body.
14	Do at least 5 minutes of this breathing. This is an essential tool for you before any activity in this book.
15	By slowly inhaling, holding and exhaling, it helps to bring our brain waves into a lower frequency state such as Alpha or Theta.
16	The frequency of the breath is approximately 0.1 HZ which is 6 cycles per minute. The frequency of 0.1 HZ helps to induce heart brain coherence.
17	You can use a timer for this breathing exercise.
18	When you are ready, do the visualization activities.

Get ready to play the very first music of your heart to attract a new lover, soul mate or twin flame.

Chapter 2 Ex-1 MANIFESTATION OF A BLISSFUL RELATIONSHIP

1	Now close your eyes, relax and visualize anything that means LOVE to you…a symbol, such as a heart, a red beautiful full-bloomed rose, or your partner's smiley face.
2	Imagine this image shining in your heart.
3	You are feeling the sensation throughout your body as the image shines even brighter and brighter with each passing moment.
4	Around your heart's region, the whole body is shining, the nerves, the cells, even the blood.
5	Take your time. Do this visualization slowly and feel the sensations sweetly for at least 5 minutes.
6	Feel the sensations getting stronger each time you visualize the image.
7	If your mind wanders, let it be and Smile. Relax and restart. Focus on the shining image and the feeling of sweet sensations throughout the body once again.
8	Continue feeling the blissful sensations in your whole body.
9	Pay attention to your heart. Inside your chest, there is a heart that is ready to get loaded with blissful sensations.
10	Generate the feeling of appreciation, gratitude, care and compassion.
11	The sensations have overtaken your soul and especially your heart, as it lightens up with bliss and love.
12	Your heart is broadcasting signals to the universe.
13	It gives and receives vibrations that resonate and attract souls just like the electromagnetic field.
14	Now imagine the image in your heart is splitting out tiny images of itself. These tiny images are small like tear drops and are filling up the space inside and outside of your body.
15	These images are now filling the space of your body inside and outside with the blissful sensation of LOVE, BLISS, JOY and GRATEFULNESS.
16	Do this visualization for at least 5 minutes.
17	Once you feel satisfied and blissful with the visualization and feeling of sensation, open your eyes gradually but NOT completely.

18	Have gaze of a very drowsy person. Eyelids are half-open & half-closed.
19	Imagine the same image shining in front of you.
20	Now hum the first few tunes of your favorite song and feel the music vibrating inside and outside the space of your body.
21	Now imagine you are entering into a new life with your beloved and feel the blissful sensations.
22	Say thank you to that source for manifesting what you want for you.
23	Say your words of gratitude once again from the core of your heart and feel the sensations with it.
24	Now, open your eyes gradually, slowly and completely. Do your best to carry this same kind of feeling when you go about your daily activities.
25	Whenever you sit, walk, stand or lay down, do your best to remember these feelings and feel the sensations of LOVE, BLISS, JOY, ECSTASY and THANKFULNESS.
26	When you are doing this activity with a partner, embrace your partner and feel each other's breath and heart beats for at least 5 minutes.
27	Look into your partner's eye and say "I am grateful to you for doing this activity with me"

Notes and Variations:

1	Grab some paper and coloring tools in your hand to draw your image or symbol practically.
2	You can place the symbol you created by hand somewhere you want to see it.
3	Make a note of gratitude next to your symbol. Example: I am grateful for everything the UNIVERSE has brought me.
4	You can hang the symbol and note on your wall, doorknob, desk, bathroom, anywhere.
5	The goal is to have gratitude all the time in every moment, so that what you want to manifest is a DONE DEAL, here and now already.
6	Keep it a complete secret. You can also place the symbol in a spot that is hidden from others. Example: below your pillow or behind your bathroom mirror. It is only between you and the source of creation.
7	Every night before going to bed and every morning after waking up are the best times to do these activities. During this period, your brain is at a lower frequency.

8	In the beginning, we suggest that you spend a minimum of 15 minutes a day on this activity and gradually extend it to 45 minutes daily.
9	You can create a script using your voice on a recorder along with your favorite music.

Chapter 3 Ex-2 SELF KNOWING PROJECT

You can try this on yourself alone or with your partner.

Follow these steps. You need to have access to a computer.

1	Take a close-up photo of your face
2	Copy the left side of your face and flip the copy vertically and paste it so that the image turns into a perfectly symmetrical face.
3	Similarly, do that for the right side of your face.
4	Similarly, you can do that for your partner's face.
5	Here, your left side of the face is a projection of your right brain
6	And the right side of the face is a projection of your left brain
7	This is how the projection works. Either side of our brain controls the opposite side of your body
8	Take a moment to sense how you feel when you see the symmetrical faces of yourselves and your partner's of each side, left and right.
9	Invite your partner to witness the mirror images.
10	There must be some gut feeling that leads you to your partner and vice versa. Observe your sensation. Can you describe it? Where? How? What?
11	Relax and take some time to recognize which side of your face and your partner's face you prefer to look at
12	What is the reason behind your specific preference for the image?
13	You have the reason and answer within yourself. Take note of that. Preferably, keep a journal and write that down.
14	Also, try morphing the left symmetrical face to the right symmetrical face.
15	You can use a future baby face prediction site. Use the left and right face photos as your parents.
16	This makes an image in between the left and right sides of your face images.
17	This complete balance is the middle-ground for you to strive for.
18	Invite your partner to do the same.
19	This project can be fun and gives you deep insight into your conscious and unconscious.
20	Most couples' faces and expressions converge as time goes by.
21	You can put this left and right morphed perfectly symmetrical face in your altar or your vision board. This is a candidate for a perfected version of you. Wonder why Buddha and Jesus's faces are always perfectly symmetrical ?

Chapter 3 Ex-3 SELF-FLOWING MOVEMENT

To carry out this self-mismatched movement activity, it is important to understand that it is a challenge for human beings to show two contradicting and opposing movements at the same time, for example, scratching their neck and rubbing their own back with vertical and horizontal movement simultaneously. Such a situation is referred to as self-mismatched movements.

Right now is the time to go through an activity of mismatched movement. It helps to balance the left-right brain and makes the unconscious more available to the conscious.

Now Prepare yourself in a completely comfortable posture by restfully sitting on a chair.

1	Stretch out both hand and squeeze both feet
2	Squeeze both hands and stretch out both feet
3	Stretch out right hand and right foot and squeeze left hand and left foot
4	Stretch out left hand and left foot and squeeze right hand and right foot
5	Stretch out right hand and squeeze the rest of your hands and feet
6	Squeeze the right hand and stretch out the rest of your hands and feet
7	Stretch out left hand and squeeze the rest of your hands and feet
8	Squeeze the left hand and stretch out the rest of your hands and feet
9	Stretch out right foot and squeeze the rest of your hands and feet
10	Squeeze the right foot and stretch out the rest of your hands and feet
11	Stretch out left foot and squeeze the rest of your hands and feet
12	Squeeze the left foot and stretch out the rest of your hands and feet
13	Stretch out right hand and left foot and squeeze left hand and right foot
14	Stretch out left hand and right foot and squeeze right hand and left foot
15	Stretch out all feet and hands
16	Squeeze all feet and hands

Notes and Variations:

1	You can sit on a chair with legs crossed and repeat the same sequence.
2	You can sit on a chair with arms crossed and repeat the same sequence.
3	Sit on a chair with both arms and legs crossed. Repeat the sequence.
4	You can synchronize your breath with the movement. Example: Breath in, Stretch out all feet and hands. Breathe out, Squeeze all feet and hands .
5	You can sit on or lay on the floor instead of a chair.
6	You can extend this activity in combination with a variety of yoga poses

	like cow and cat postures.
7	For example, stretch out the left (right) arm and right (left) leg in cat pose. With number 13(14) above.
8	Set aside time for yourself to try this activity. It can take you a few trials and errors.
9	Game idea Number One: One partner can call out the sequence randomly. He or she will also keep the score. Take turns.
10	Game idea Number Two: The partners sit facing each other. One is the leader and one is the follower. The leader stretches out or/and squeezes his or her fingers randomly. The number added up between the leader and follower from the stretched out fingers CANNOT be zero or greater than 10. If it is, the leader earns one point. Take Turns.
11	Game idea Number Three: Similar to Game idea Number two, but use toes instead.
12	Game idea Number Four: Similar to Game idea Number two, but use both fingers and toes. (See Photos.)

Chapter 3 Ex-4 MIRROR AND FLOWING WITH PARTNER

1	Sit facing each other
2	Assign the roles of a leader and a follower to you and your partner
3	The leader signals the other using some movement of the body including raising hands, stretching feet and rubbing the chest, etc.
4	The one who copies must do the same in front of the partner no matter what.
5	Close hands, open fists and do whatever you both like for example pick your nose with your thumb and then suck your thumb. Be creative and playful
6	Continue for 12 rounds or 5 minutes.
7	This is a form of non-verbal communication between you and your partner.
8	Congratulate yourself for being in alignment with your partner in the end
9	Have a big hug and feel each other's breath and heart beats for at least 5 minutes after the session.
10	Remember to look into your partner's eye and say "I am grateful to you for doing this activity with me"

Notes and Variations:

1	Do the opposite side as the leader. Example: Leader's left arm stretches out and follower's right arm stretches out.
2	Play the follower's most hated piece of music during this activity to distract him or her.
3	Do this activity in different groups. Example: standing, sitting, laying down.
4	Try it with both partners with eyes closed with verbal instructions only. Then open your eyes to see if you both are on a similar track.
5	Note that communication happens in non-verbal and non-visual dimensions too.
6	Take a few deep breaths and look into each other's eyes between each round. See if the follower and leader can communicate telepathically about the next movement with eyes closed.

7	You can make it more challenging by adding more details and variations to the activity. Example: yoga poses such as Sun, Moon or Earth salutations.
8	Video record you and your partners.
9	Try movements that you rarely do. Example: The leader writes a word with the left toes and the follower does the same with the right toes.
10	With each movement, experience bodily sensations that are linked with it.
11	Congratulations to each other in the end. Example: "Thanks for letting me win" or "Thanks for entertaining me."

Figure 25. Game idea Number Four Photo 1

Figure 26. Game idea Number Four Photo 2

Chapter 4 Ex-5 MIND-BUILDING WITH YOUR EYES

Have you noticed that whenever we have a distracting thought, our eyes start moving unconsciously? If you ever observe a sharpshooter aim at the target, most often than not, the eye of focus would not blink at all. In fact, gazing at an image or an object for a prolonged period is a proven method to train the mind. This skill can transfer to any situation when laser sharp concentration is required. The image we use is the mandala of 231 gates from the book of Sefer Yetzirah. The book is considered one of the important books of the mystical Jewish Kabbalist traditions. It is said that these Kabbalah syllables are seeds of creation. They have magical powers. Dan Winter and Stan Tenen both show that the Jewish letters are 2D projections of a Torus Vortex, which is the fundmental unit of our creation, the atom. Vincent Bridges states that the Ophanic alphabet, which is similar to the Hebrew alphabet, can be used in magic spells.

1	Simply stare at the center point of the image.
2	Do your best to minimize Blinking.
3	Set a timer for 5 minutes, staring at the center dot.
4	After the timer is up, close your eyes and visualize the image in the middle of your forehead for the duration of 12 breaths.
5	After the 12 breaths, slowly open your eyes with a diverse gaze. Just receive and don't project for another 12 breaths, before resuming normal activity.
6	Increase by one minute per week, up to 20 minutes, for the open eye staring time
7	You might see other images depending on the internal state of your being.

Figure 27. 231 gates Mandala from Sefer Yetzirah

Chapter 4 Ex-6 FACING-YOURSELF

This activity can be done as a preparatory step for the activity in this chapter. It helps with knowing, loving and having compassion with yourself, the most important character in YOUR story.

1	Find a space that has a mirror and ideally, where the lighting intensity can be controlled.
2	Now make yourself comfortable, make sure your space is brightly lit.
3	Set a timer and gaze at the mirror into your eyes for 5 minutes.
4	After that, dim the light. Gaze at the mirror into your eyes for 5 minutes.
5	Stay in front of the mirror, imagine a point about the length from your shoulder to your middle finger, beyond the mirror. Stare at that imaginary point for 5 minutes
6	Notice the changes in your mirror image, your sensations, feelings, thoughts and emotions.
7	Just observe and relax. Let it be.
8	If your mind wanders, smile and relax.
9	Start again with a renewed and relaxed focus.
10	You might see images other than the known image of yourselves. It depends on the internal state of your being.
11	Relax and have a feeling of Gratitude. Have Compassion and Love of whatever images you observe during the process. Loving yourself is the first step of loving kindness.
12	Keep a journal and write down what you observed and your feelings after the session.

Notes and Variations:

1	You can focus on just one eye at a time and rotate.
2	Example: for the first 5 minutes, focus on the left eye and for the second five minutes, focus on the right eye.
3	You can focus on an imaginary point that is one to two palm widths (thumb to pinky) above and between the middle of eyebrows. Play with the distance and find one that is comfortable for you.
4	You can use your palm to cover one eye and only use one to do the exercise.
5	If time is a constraint, pick only one configuration and rotate on different days.
6	Example: Use a bright light one day and use dim light on the other day.
7	Example: Try dim light on an imaginary point.
8	Example: Try bright light on an imaginary point.
9	Mix and match the possible combinations of eyes, focus points and light intensity
10	You might observe different images of your face manifesting in different eyes, focus points and lighting configurations.
11	Repeat the cycle of using the same configuration for 30 days, if one particular configuration resonates with you.

Chapter 4 Ex-7 FACING YOURSELF WITH A PARTNER

1	Sit on a couch with your partner, facing each other side by side.
2	Observe your breathing as it comes naturally.
3	Now scan your body and visualize your cells are relaxed and smiling at you.
4	Start a timer, set it for 5 minutes.
5	Each partner covers one eye with their palm, rests their elbow on the back of the couch and stares into your partners' uncovered eye
6	You might observe your partner's face is transforming.
7	Let it be and relax. Keep the focus on your partner's uncovered eye.
8	When the timer is up, gradually and slowly diffuse your vision to include your surroundings.
9	Hold each other's hands and relax and breathe deeply together.
10	Repeat for the other eyes.
11	Repeat for both eyes without any covering.
12	Now, put your right hand on your partner's heart and your left hand on

	top of your partner's right hand which is on your heart.
13	Smile at your partner and look into your partner's eyes.
14	Say it slowly and clearly.
15	"I am grateful to you for doing this activity with me".
16	Feel that sensation of gratefulness throughout the body especially in the heart.
17	Have a big hug and feel each other's breath and heart beat for at least 5 minutes.
18	Whatever image you see, it is an internal projection of your own onto your partner's face. Have Compassion and Love of whatever images you observe during the process. Loving yourself is the first step of loving your partner.

Notes and Variations:

1	You and your partner can lay side by side facing each other for this exercise.
2	According to Tibetan Buddhism, the right eye projects and the left eye receives. This way, you both can project and receive each other's view and energy.
3	Focus on a point on the top of your partner's head.
4	Imagine a point about the length of the shoulder to the tip of the middle finger beyond your partner's forehead and gaze at that imaginary point.
5	Keep a journal together and draw the images observed on your partner's face and the sensations, feelings, emotions and thoughts evoked.

Chapter 5 Ex-8 TUNE INTO THE FORCE

This activity is a version of the Tai Chi Zhang Zhong. It is one of the most important foundations in Chi Gong. This activity's goal is to cultivate and grow our life force Chi field by harmonizing and resonating the inner field with the outer field. The bigger the field you have, the higher the intensity of the bliss you can experience and the more people will get attracted to you. The main point of awareness of this practice is directed toXia Dan Tian's point. In Chinese, it translates to Lower Elixir Field. It is the center of gravity or very close to the center of gravity for most humans.

Let's have a feel where Xia Dan Tian is:

1	Close your fingers.
2	Put your thumb on your navel with your palm cupping on your belly.
3	Bring awareness to where your ring finger is, right below your navel.
4	Now, from this point, have your mind's eye go deeply into your body.
5	Go very deep, until it almost touches the front surface of your spine.
6	This is where Xia Dan Tian is.
7	Remember where this point is, the Xia Dan Tian.

Now love yourself enough to set aside 10 minutes. Set your timer.

1	Stand in a neutral position.
2	Position your feet slightly wider than your hip distance.
3	Slightly bend your knees.
4	Observe your knees, make sure they stay a little bouncy and relaxed.
5	Now, close your eyes.
6	You can pretend you are holding an Imaginary Chi Basket Ball and this Ball is touching your belly lovingly.
7	Put your awareness on the Xia Dan Tian Point.
8	Here, the line of gravity is aligned with the spine naturally.
9	Imagine the top of your head is hanging by an imaginary Chi Rope.
10	Allow your spine to extend naturally towards mother earth.
11	Slightly squeeze your buttocks.
12	Slightly tilt your tailbone inward.
13	You can imagine there is a chair behind you.
14	Only your tailbone is slightly touching this imaginary chair.
15	The center of gravity is passing through your heels in this position.
16	You can imagine the weight is distributed more towards the heel.

17	Slightly squeeze your shoulder blades.
18	Open the chest.
19	Relax the shoulders.
20	Imagine a picture of you when you were 3 years old.
21	Can you mimic this 3-year-old self of yours.?
22	This child has such ease and grace of action.
23	Continue breathing naturally.
24	Relax your facial muscles.
25	Relax your whole jaw and throat. Put a slight smile on your face.
26	Your cells are smiling back at you.
27	Now, slightly raise your tongue and have the tip of your tongue touching the upper front teeth' backside.
28	Now put a relaxed focus on the Xia Dan Tian.
29	If your mind wanders, just relax and smile.
30	Bring back your relaxed focus on the Xia Dan Tian.
31	When the timer is up, open your eyes slowly and gradually.
32	Just receive and don't project/
33	Lower your arms and straighten your knees slowly.
34	Take a few deep relaxing breaths.

Notes and Variations:

1	You can gradually build up endurance by adding one more minute per week, up to 60 minutes.
2	If you feel your body is lacking in strength, relax, and come out from the position into a natural standing position. Start with 2 minutes and build up gradually. Slow and steady wins the race.
3	If you observe there are sensations in your palms, fingers, feet, and toes, then that is good, your Chi is moving and growing. Nevertheless, keep the focus on the Xia Dan Tian.
4	You might observe sensations in different points of your body, but keep your focus on the Xia Dan Tian.
5	Doing it barefootin an outdoor setting is the best. You can experiment with different outdoor settings.
6	The morning dew=s on the grass is considered very healing and so is the sand on the beach.
7	Doing it barefoot facilitates an exchange with the field of mother earth, which is the most abundant source of negative ions.
8	You can also do it next to a tree.
9	The tree's force field is very healing. Again remember the plot of

	Avatar?
10	You can experiment with doing the exercise with your back facing the early morning sun or mild afternoon sun. Early morning sun is considered the most nourishing.
11	According to Chinese Medicine, Yang is known as the positively charged energy field. The backside of the body is considered yang. If you observe how most creatures operate in nature, they all have their backside facing the sun. As the morning sun is growing, it's more beneficial than the evening sun which is declining. However, some sun is better than no sun.
12	If you do it indoors, try it at different places as the energy field indoors can be constructive or destructive, it depends. You have to experiment and go with the flow.
13	Keep a journal and keep track of how you feel differently in different spaces and times when you do this activity

Shoulders Relax. Inside Arms and Legs
Relax the Groins. The four fingers are
Thumb and Index finger is circular. Be s
the best you can. Imagine a Chi Ball of
are embracing and it is kissing your be

Figure 28. Tai Chi Zhang Zhong Image 1

Have the spine erect in natural posi[tion]
like a child. Relax the stomach , t[he]
belly and the shoulders. Visualize [the]
legs and feet are like tree and rooted [into]
mother earth. Tug the chin and have [the]
tongue touching the backside of t[he]
upper front teeth. Put the awarenes[s]
Xia Dan Tian

Figure 29. Tai Chi Zhang Zhong Image 2

Figure 30. Tai Chi Zhang Zhong Image 3

Chapter 5 Ex-9 TUNE INTO THE FORCE WITH A PARTNER

1	Choose a relaxed space, for example, a park, beachside or a quiet room.
2	You and your partner start by standing very close, facing each other.
3	You can use the distance of the tip of the middle finger to the elbow of the shorter partner as the measurement.
4	Now,repeat the Tai Chi Zhang Zhong for each partner.
5	You and your partner's palms are facing opposite sides of each other, but NOT touching.
6	Example: the front side of Kash's left palmis facing the backside of Moorea's right palm.
7	The front side of Moorea's left palm is facing the backside of Kash's right palm.
8	Continue in this posture for 5-10 minutes at a time using the protocol of the Tai Chi Zhang Zhong.
9	Switch the intertwined orientation for another 5-10 minutes.
10	There are four configurations with this left and right palms position. You and your partner should be able to figure it out as an exercise.
11	When finished, remember to look into your partner's eyes and Say:
12	"I am very grateful to you for doing this activity with me."
13	Have a big hug and feel each other's breath and heart beats for at least 5 minutes.

Notes and Variations:

1	One of the partners can place a hand on top like patting a child's head or holding it. The other partner can have the palms face up like they're receiving a gift.
2	Preferably, the receiving and giving palms positions need to be done for each other. As in any healthy relationship, the give and take needs to be balanced. As you and your partner resonate with this practice, make sure the configurations of the hands are balanced.
3	You and your partners can experiment with intertwining each other's legs, similar to salsa dancing.
4	If you can find a thin enough tree, you and your partner can embrace and hold hands with the tree in the middle. If NOT, simply visualizing you and your partner are expanding and merging with the tree in the middle.
5	Observe and remember the sensations in your body. BLISS, WARMTH, pain, relief, lightness, heaviness or whatever feelings you have during the session

6	Observe and remember if any emotions are evoked like LOVE, JOY, sadness or depression or whatever moods you have during the session
7	Observe how both of you feel after doing this activity, for example, energized or exhausted.
8	Keep a journal and write down all these feelings, images, thoughts, sensations, and emotions into the journal for future reference.

Figure 31. Partners Tai Chi Zhang Zhong Photo 1

Figure 32. Partners Tai Chi Zhang Zhong Phtoto 2

Figure 33. Partners Tai Chi Zhang Zhong with Tree

This is an activity for providing love and care to our body systems via our chakras, our personal energy vortex blackhole in our mini-Universe. Our body is the most marvelous machine in the universe. In fact, our body is wishing and wanting to give us the most abundant and radiant energy possible, provided that we give it what it needs for its job. It takes anywhere between 20-60 minutes.

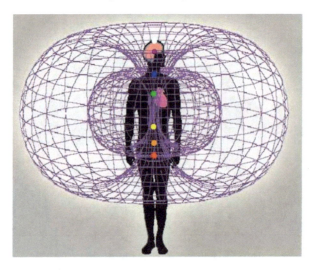

Figure 34. Our Aura forms a Vortex Torus ?

1	Sit comfortably in a chair or on the floor.
2	Inhale once slowly and deeply. Hold for a moment and Exhale.
3	Let the relaxation come into your body.
4	Put your focus on your first chakra, which is located at the center of your perineum.
5	You can imagine breathing in and out from the center of your perineum.
6	Focus on safety, security, love, gratitude, joy, bliss, or any positive feeling, while observing the sensation in your first chakra.
7	Repeat the breath and observation of sensation and positive emotion for another five cycles of breath on your first chakra.
8	Move your awareness to the second chakra which is about two fingers-width above your pubic bone deep within your body.
9	You can imagine you are breathing in and out from the second chakra.

10	Inhale slowly and deeply. Hold for a moment. Exhale slowly and Deeply. Relax.
11	Focus on passion, excitement, virtuality, love, bliss, joy, gratitude, or any positive feeling, while observing the sensation in your second chakra.
12	Repeat the breath and observation of sensation and positive emotion for another five cycles of breath on your second chakra.
13	Now move your awareness to the third chakra which is deep within your navel, kissing the front part of your spine.
14	You can imagine you are breathing in through your Navel Chakra.
15	Inhale slowly and deeply. Hold for a moment. Exhale slowly and Deeply. Relax.
16	Focus on self-confidence, will power love, bliss, joy, gratitude, or any positive feeling while observing the sensation in your third chakra.
17	Repeat the breath and observation of sensation and positive emotion for another five cycles of breath on your third chakra.
18	Now move your awareness to the fourth chakra, which is where your heart is about to kiss your spine.
19	You can imagine that you are breathing in through the heart chakra.
20	Inhale slowly and deeply. Hold for a moment. Exhale slowly and Deeply. Relax.
21	Focus on Altruistic giving and service, love, bliss, joy, gratitude or any positive feeling while observing the sensation in your fourth chakra.
22	Repeat the breath and observation of sensation and positive emotion for another five cycles of breath on your fourth chakra.
23	Now move your awareness to the fifth chakra which is where your neck meets your torso,deep within your body.
24	You can imagine you are breathing in through your throat chakra.
25	Inhale slowly and deeply. Hold for a moment. Exhale slowly and Deeply. Relax.
26	Focus on openness, truthfulness, love, bliss, joy, gratitude, or any positive feeling while observing the sensation in your fifth chakra.
27	Repeat the breath and observation of sensation and positive emotion for another five cycles of breath on your fifth chakra.
28	Now move your awareness to the sixth chakra, the third eye chakra.
29	You can imagine three lines. The first line is straight across from the tops of your ears, the second line is from the midpoint of your eyebrows, straight back and the third line goes from the top of your skull straight down. The point where these three lines meet is where your third eye chakra is.
30	Imagine you are breathing in and out through the third eye chakra.
31	Inhale slowly deeply. Hold for a moment. Exhale slowly deeply. Relax.
32	Focus on silence, stillness, love, bliss, joy, gratitude or any positive feeling

	while observing the sensation in your sixth chakra.
33	Repeat the breath and observation of sensation and positive emotion for another two cycles of breath on your sixth chakra.
34	Now move your awareness to the seventh chakra which is the highest point of your skull.
35	You can imagine you are breathing in through the seventh chakra.
36	Inhale slowly and deeply. Hold for a moment. Exhale slowly and Deeply. Relax.
37	Focus on freedom, light, love, joy, bliss, gratitude, or any positive feeling while observing the sensation in your seventh chakra.
38	Repeat the breath and observation of sensation and positive emotion for another five cycles of breath on your seventh chakra.
39	You have completed the basic form of chakra meditation.

Chapter 6 Ex-11 VORTEX MEDITATION SECOND FORM

1	This builds up from the first form. The only difference is that we expand our sphere of awareness into space. This space is about the size and shape of a donut inside of our body. We observe this space and the sensation. We are breathing through the chakra points.

Chapter 6 Ex-12 VORTEX MEDITATION THIRD FORM

1	This builds from the second form. We expand our sphere of awareness into space, the size and shape of a giant Glitter Swim Ring float, which is about the radius of an out-stretched arm beyond our physical body. We observe this space and any sensation in it, inside and outside of our body. We are breathing through the chakra points.
2	After meditating on all the chakras on our physical body, we can meditate on a point that is one arm width above the top of our head in space, using the same protocol. Breath in. Hold. Breath out. Observe and feel positive emotions. This point is the KA point of Egyptian spiritual practice.
3	Imagine that all the physical chakras, including the KA point, have created a glitter swim ring float stack and they each connect and merge with each other in space. Focus on this volume of space created by the stack of

chakras as a whole unit.

Notes and Variations:

1 You can visualize the color of the rainbow at each Chakra

For example: red for root chakra at the premium, tailbone and pubic bone, orange for sacral chakra between the pubic bone and navel, yellow for solar plexus chakra at the belly button, green for heart chakra near the heart in the middle of the chest, blue for throat chakra in the neck where we find the protruding of the Adam's apple, purple for third eye chakra in the center of our head and white for the crown chakra at the top of the
2 head.

Let's talk about the theory behind it.

As discussed in the previous chapter, our unconscious can tell us what is TRUEor FALSE very accurately. As a result, whenever we state a TRUE statement to be FALSE or VICE VERSA, there is an agreement or disagreement of the conscious and subconscious mind. This conflict can boost or hamper energy flow. Recall how stress can diminish our bio-field in the previous chapter. Whenever we are in conflict, we are in fact in stress. As a result, our bio-field diminishes and weakens when we are in conflict and vice versa. This leads to either weakening or strengthening of a muscle.

Moorea the Author says: "My first muscle test was done when I was transitioning to a vegan diet. I had doubts about eating rice, even though I really like eating it. However, I was on a low budget to get any tests done. So, I did the muscle test on the statement, "Rice is good for me", and on the potential substitute, "Quinoa is GOOD for me." The muscle test showed my strength weakening after saying the "RICE" statement and my muscle strength boosted when I said the "QUINOA" statement. I trusted the test, so I quit eating rice and started eating quinoa instead. Immediately after the transition, I felt better with my body and got more energy. A couple of years later, I did a food allergy test and it indeed showed that RICE is NOT good for my body, and QUINOA is good for my body."

Now, we need to have the baseline muscle test for a known true fact to calibrate further testing of TRUE or FALSE statements.

1	The test subject is standing naturally and relaxed
2	The test subject has the dominant arm stretched out horizontally, palm facing down
3	The test subject says out aloud a known TRUE statement, holding the position. The best TRUE statement is some activity, thing or person that one TRULY LOVES. Example: "I LOVE MY MOM."
4	Slowly, the tester applies force to the subject's out-stretched arm vertically and attempts to lower the test subject's arm. Simultaneously, the test subject resists, attempting to keep the out-stretched arm horizontal and to continue holding the position.
5	Is the test subject's arm firm and able to resist the lowering force? If Yes, proceed to the next step, otherwise, have the test subject lower the arm, relax and then repeat the steps. (Note: if the subject's arm cannot be firm after a few repeated tests, his or her field may be reversed, or his or her

	deep unconscious self is NOT loving that activity or thing).
6	Now, the test subject says out aloud a known FALSE statement. The best FALSE statement is some activity, thing or person that one TRULY HATES, but states the opposite. Example: I hate mosquitoes biting me, so I'd say, "I LOVE MOSQUITOS BITING ME."
7	Slowly, the tester applies force to the subject's out-stretched arm vertically and attempts to lower the test subject's arm. Simultaneously, the test subject resists to keep the out-stretched arm horizontal, keeping the position
8	Is the test subject's arm weak and NOT able to resist the lowering force? If Yes, then the test is completed and serves as a baseline. Otherwise, have the test subject lower the arm, relax and then repeat the steps. (Note: if the subject's arm cannot be weakened after a few repeated tests, his or her field may either be reversed or his or her deep unconscious self is NOT hating that activity or thing)
9	The ability to resist the test giver's application of force will significantly decrease. The subject might have the outstretched arm lowered immediately after the tester's application of force.

After the calibration, we have a feeling of what TRUE and FALSE statements do to the test subject's strength of muscle via enhancing or hampering energy flow. There is a very small percentage of people who muscle tests will NOT work on because their field is reversed. Fixing it is beyond the scope of this book.

Chapter 6 Ex-14 PARTNER ENERGY VORTEX CHECKING:

1	The test subject is standing naturally and relaxing.
2	The test subject has one arm stretched out horizontally, palm facing down.
3	The test subject puts the other palm on the front side of the body's closest chakra proximity. For the first chakra, the palm can be put on the tailbone. For the sixth chakra, the palm can be put on the forehead.
4	Example: For checking the third chakra, the test subject puts his or her palm on the navel.
5	The test subject says out aloud the statement concerning the chakra.
6	Example: My navel chakra is balanced.
7	Slowly, the tester applies force to the subject's out-stretched arm vertically and attempts to lower the test subject's arm. Simultaneously, the test subject is resisting to keep the out-stretched arm horizontal and to keep the position.

8	If the statement is TRUE, then the test subject's outstretched arm resistance would stay firm and remain horizontal.
9	If the statement is FALSE, then the test subject's outstretched arm would become weak and drop.
10	Do this for all the chakras and keep a record of the results.

After all the chakras are done on the front side of the body, we can now proceed to the backside of the body. Repeat the steps on the front side. The difference is the test subject does NOT put his or her palm on his or her own chakra. Instead, the tester puts his or her palm on the test subject's backside of the body's chakra. For the first chakra, the palm is on the tailbone. For the sixth chakra, the palm is on the area where the spine enters the skull. For example, the navel chakra is on the vertebrate across the navel. If the test contradicts with the first set of tests, it implies that the tester's energy field is helping to balance or unbalance the test subject's field. For example, if the navel chakra is balanced in the front test and then becomes unbalanced in the back test, it implies that the tester's field is making the test subject's field unbalanced and vice versa.

1) Say a true statement

if the statement is true, the
muscle tends to get stronger
because of more energy flow.

and vice versa.

so we have the baseline

2) Tester applies force

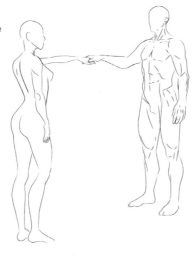

Tester puts palm on the back chakra
point and subject says e.g. My navel
chakra is balance. If it is True. Arm will
hold up or vice versa

Subject puts palm on the front chakra
point says e.g. my nevel chakra is
blance. If it true. Arm will hold up or vice versa

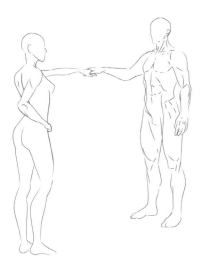

Figure 37. Muscle Test for Energy Vortex Points

Chapter 6 Ex-15 PARTNER VORTEX ENERGY HEALING

1	You and your partner need to complete the Chakra Checking activities.
2	Identify the imbalanced chakra in your body and in your partner's body from the completed Chakra Checking activities. Only work with those chakras that show the balancing effect from your partner.
3	Stand facing each other.
4	Look into each other's eyes, about to hug each other.
5	Ask permission from your partner before proceeding further as an acknowledgement of the divinity in him or her.
6	Swing your head to your right which is your partner's left. Your partner does the same thing as you and your partner's left chest wants to touch each other. We want a heart-to-heart hug.

7	Place your right hand on your partner's most imbalanced chakra. Your partner will do the same thing for you. (Note: If the back muscle test showed that your partner would only make your chakra unbalanced, then you two need to do more investigation to find out the root causes. This investigation is beyond the scope of this book.)
8	Put your left hand freely on your partner's back using your intuition.
9	Relax and Inhale slowly and deeply. Hold for a moment. Exhale slowly and Deeply,
10	Feel the hug and feel the sensations throughout the body.
11	Focus on Love, Joy, Freedom, Bliss, Gratitude and other highly elated emotions, sensations and vibrations.
12	Hold this position for 5 minutes.
13	After the activity, remember to look into your partner's eyes and say, "I am grateful to you for doing this activity with me and sharing your time with me".

Notes and Variations:

1	Play the game "TRUTH OR DARE " and use the muscle test to verify if your partner is really truthful or NOT.
2	Experiment this activity with different hand configurations. An example is to place both hands on the same most imbalanced chakra. Both hands on the most imbalanced chakra.
3	Share any emotions, sensations, thoughts and images related to this activity with your partner.
4	Keep a journal and record how you feel for future reference.

Yogic practice suggests the sound "A", "U", "M" is the most fundamental sound a human can make. It says that this is the sound we hear during the ultimate ecstatic mystical experience. All other sounds are created based on these three fundamental sounds, plus the movement of our tongue, throat, lips, and jaws. The "A" sound signifies the lower realm which is the dimension of mineral rocks, plants, animals and ghosts. The "U" sound signifies the middle realm, which is the dimension of human and other humanoids. The "M" sound signifies the higher realm which is the dimension for being evolved past the need of having a physical body, like angels and Celestial Beings. The three sounds combined signify the whole of creation and THE SILENCE is the sound which is beyond. It's always in the HERE and NOW. The NO-Thing is in Everything.

Follow these steps:

1	Sit comfortably on a chair or on the floor.
2	Make sure the spine is erect and the body is relaxed.
3	Take a few deep breaths
4	Relax and inhale deeply, open your mouth, relax the jaw and tongue, and say "AAA…" while focusing on the area below the navel deep into the torso.
5	Slowly close the mouth. Have the sound and awareness travel up along the torso to the sternum area between the nipples, and make the sound "UUU"
6	Slowly, further close the mouth. Have the sound and awareness travel up along the torso to the throat area, and make the sound "MMM"
7	Slowly feel the sound vibration and awareness travel up to the area between your ears and behind your eyebrows.
8	When the exhale breath is finished with the humming, simply relax and let go. Observe the silence. Pause for as much time as possible until you need to inhale another breath. This is one cycle.
9	Do this humming for a minimum of 5 minutes
10	Increase one minute per week, to a maximum of 30 minutes.

Chapter 7 Ex-16 KABBALAH CUBE CHANTING.

This is a practice that comes from the tradition of Kabbalah of Sefer Yetzirah, one of the most important works on Jewish mysticism. We are using the seed syllables of creation "He, Yod, Vau". The Sefer Yetzirah says that THE CREATOR uses these three letters to create everything in the beginning.

Follow these steps:

1	Sit facing North or East comfortably in a chair or on the floor with your spine erected.
2	Use the breath to claim your mind.
3	Just a refresher: it is simply done with ratio breathing of 4:1:4:1
4	Breathe in for a count of 4 seconds. Hold for 1 second and then Exhale for 4 seconds and hold for 1 second.
5	Do this ratio breathing to calm the mind and relax the body for about 12 breaths or 5 minutes.
6	Once the body is relaxed and the mind is calm, take a deep relaxed breath.
7	Chant "Yod, He, Vau " and visualize the sound vibrations moving upward and beyond as far as you can with your imagination.
8	Pause for a moment and take another deep relaxed breath.
9	Chant "Yod, Vau, He "and visualize the sound energy moving downward and beyond as far as you can with your imagination.
10	Pause for a moment and take another deep relaxed breath.
11	Chant "He, Yod, Vau" and visualize the sound vibrations moving forward and beyond as far as you can with your imagination.
12	Pause for a moment and take another deep relaxed breath.
13	Chant "Vau, He, Yod" and visualize the sound vibrations moving backward and beyond as far as you can with your imagination.
14	Pause for a moment and take another deep relaxed breath.
15	Chant "Vau, Yod, He" and visualize the sound vibrations moving right and beyond as far as you can with your imagination.
16	Pause for a moment and take another deep relaxed breath.
17	Chant "He, Vau, Yod" and visualize the sound vibrations moving left and beyond as far as you can with your imagination.
18	Once all six directions are done, put your awareness on the Heart Chakra and sit and relax for a moment.
19	Take another deep and relaxed breath and chant "YOD HE VAU HE".
20	Pause and just observe the sensations on the Heart Chakra.
21	This is one cycle. Do at least 3 cycles.
22	When it is all done, slowly open the eyes. Just receive and don't project. Gaze into space.

| 23 | Take another few breaths before resuming the normal focus of your eyes and regular activities. |

Chapter 7 Ex-17 PARTNER SOUND HEALING.

Dan Winter and Stéphane Cardinaux's research on golden ratio and gravity shows that each of our Chakras have a particular frequency for optimal functioning. This can be approximated by the Heptatonic music scale, such as the piano keys. In general, the lower frequencies correspond to the lower Chakras of the body and vice versa. We can use either our vocal cords, if one is confident enough, or we can use a frequency generator app. We can optionally augment with a homemade gadget from a beer can to make the vibrations more observable. If one has the ambition, one can get a tuning fork set. Activate the source vibration in close proximity to the corresponding Chakra, or physically touch it against the body. And then, at the same time, the partner chants the Sanskrit Seed Mantra for that particular Chakra. Below is the table of each Chakras' optimal frequency, according to Stéphane Cardinaux's research, along with seed mantras according to tradition.

Chakra	Frequency	Sanskrit Mantra	Piano Key
Root	119	Lam	Do, C
Sex	131	Ham	Re, D
Navel	153	Ram	Mi,E
Heart	220	Yam	Fa,F
Throat	370	Ham	Sol,G
Third Eye	760	Om	La,A
Crown	840	Ah	Ti,B

Table 1. Sound of Major Chakras

Play and see which one works for you and your partner. We suggest that you and your partner do the Chakra Muscle test before and after this activity. You and your partner can do this activity multiple times in the span of a week to build up sensitivity. Follow these steps:

Sitting	
1	Have both partners sit on a chair or on the floor facing each other.
2	Sing out the piano key or the Sanskrit Mantra on each of the Chakras for 10 seconds each.
3	Do at least 5 rounds.

Laying	

down	
1	Have the receiving partner laying down face up on a flat surface comfortably.
2	Sing out the piano key or Mantra while placing your hand on your partner's corresponding Chakra.
3	The singer has their mouth close to the particular part of the receiver's body before singing it out.
4	Sing out the Sanskrit Mantra or Piano Key for 10 seconds for all of the Chakras
5	Do at least 5 rounds.
6	Now have the receiver face down.
7	Repeat the same process
8	Remember to have a big hug and feel each other's breath and heart beats for at least 5 minutes after the session.
9	Remember to look into your partner's eye and say, "I am grateful to you for doing this with me today.

Notes and Variations:

1	One can perform the protocol on all seven chakras or focus only on those chakras that need to be more balanced. You can do the muscle test first.
2	One can purchase tuning forks for further experiments.
3	For tuning forks or other gadgets, one can use the frequency body pic shown. Experiment and Play. The frequency body is a continuum. The frequencies shown serve as a guideline.

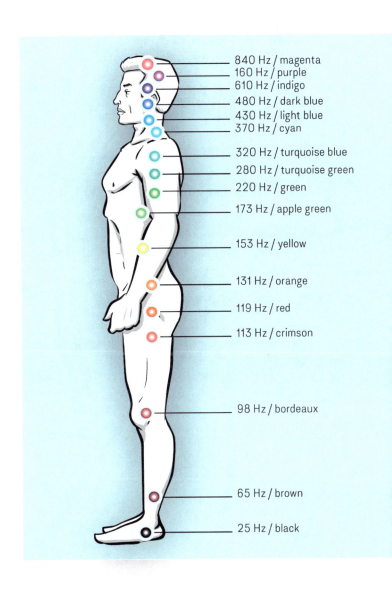

840 Hz / magenta
160 Hz / purple
610 Hz / indigo
480 Hz / dark blue
430 Hz / light blue
370 Hz / cyan

320 Hz / turquoise blue
280 Hz / turquoise green
220 Hz / green

173 Hz / apple green

153 Hz / yellow

131 Hz / orange

119 Hz / red

113 Hz / crimson

98 Hz / bordeaux

65 Hz / brown

25 Hz / black

Figure 38. Frequencies of Major Energy Vortex of average human body

Chapter 8 Ex-18 MINDFULNESS BREATH MEDITATION First variation:

1	Sit comfortable on a chair or on the floor.
2	Relax and have the spine erect naturally.
3	Observe the sensation on the nostril while the breathing is coming and going.
4	Observe the sensation on the area below the nostrils and above the upper lip while the breath is coming and going.
5	Just relax and observe.
6	Do this observation for at least 10 minutes.
7	One can increase the time duration one minute per week up to an hour.

Chapter 8 Ex-19 MINDFULNESS BREATH MEDITATION Second variation:

1	When one is comfortable with the first variation for at least 20 minutes.
2	Count the breath while staying in the observation attitude in variation one.
3	One inhale and one exhale count as one.
4	Set a target for the count. For example: 12 counts, 60 counts, 100 counts.
5	If one can keep the awareness without losing track of the count, then up level to the next target. Example from 12 counts to 24 counts.
6	We encourage you to set the goal of achieving counting to 100. If one does, one has cultivated laser sharp focus with a relaxed attitude. This quality of being will carry onto other aspects of life.

Mindfulness body meditation.

1	Now move your awareness to your left toes. Observe any sensations. Just Observe, Relax and Let go. Observe for a duration of about 3 breaths.
2	Now move your awareness to your whole left foot. Observe any sensations. Just Observe, Relax and Let go. Observe for a duration of about 3 breaths.
3	Now move your awareness to your left calf. Observe any sensations. Just Observe, Relax and Let go. Observe for a duration of about 3 breaths.
4	Now move your awareness to your left thigh. Observe any sensations. Just Observe, Relax and Let go. Observe for a duration of about 3 breaths.
5	Now move your awareness to your left groin. Observe any sensations. Just Observe, Relax and Let go. Observe for a duration of about 3 breaths.
6	Now move your awareness to your perineum, anus and sex organs. Observe any sensations. Just Observe, Relax and Let go. Observe for a duration of about 3 breaths.
7	Now move your awareness to your right groin. Observe any sensations. Just Observe, Relax and Let go. Observe for a duration of about 3 breaths.
8	Now move your awareness to your right thigh. Observe any sensations. Just Observe, Relax and Let go. Observe for a duration of about 3 breaths.
9	Now move your awareness to your right calf. Observe any sensations. Just Observe, Relax and Let go. Observe for a duration of about 3 breaths.
10	Now move your awareness to your right foot. Observe any sensations. Just Observe, Relax and Let go. Observe for a duration of about 3 breaths.
11	Now move your awareness to your right toes. Observe any sensations. Just Observe, Relax and Let go. Observe for a duration of about 3 breaths.
12	Now move your awareness to your butt Observe any sensations. Just Observe, Relax and Let go. Observe for a duration of about 3 breaths.
13	Now move your awareness to the area on your back. The area from the tip of your tailbone to the point across the navel. Observe any sensations. Just Observe, Relax and Let go. Observe for a duration of about 3 breaths.
14	Now move your awareness to the area on your back. The area from the point across the navel to the point across from your nipples. Observe any sensations. Just Observe, Relax and Let go. Observe for a duration of about 3 breaths.
15	Now move your awareness to the area on your back. The area from the point across from your nipples to the back of your throat. Observe any sensations. Just Observe, Relax and Let go. Observe for a duration of about 3 breaths.
16	Now move your awareness to the area on the back of your neck. Observe any sensations. Just Observe, Relax and Let go. Observe for a duration of about 3 breaths.
17	Now move your awareness to the area on the back of your skull. The area of your head that touches a pillow. Observe any sensations. Just Observe, Relax

	and Let go. Observe for a duration of about 3 breaths.
18	Now move your awareness to your skull, any area that has hair or there should be hair. Observe any sensations. Just Observe, Relax and Let go. Observe for a duration of about 3 breaths.
19	Now move your awareness to your forehead. Observe any sensations. Just Observe, Relax and Let go. Observe for a duration of about 3 breaths.
20	Now move your awareness to your eyebrows and eyes. Observe any sensations. Just Observe, Relax and Let go. Observe for a duration of about 3 breaths.
21	Now move your awareness to your ears. Observe any sensations. Just Observe, Relax and Let go. Observe for a duration of about 3 breaths.
22	Now move your awareness to your nose. Observe any sensations. Just Observe, Relax and Let go. Observe for a duration of about 3 breaths.
23	Now move your awareness to your cheeks. Observe any sensations. Just Observe, Relax and Let go. Observe for a duration of about 3 breaths.
24	Now move your awareness to your mouth, teeth and chin. Observe any sensations. Just Observe, Relax and Let go. Observe for a duration of about 3 breaths.
25	Now move your awareness to your throat and front part of your neck. Observe any sensations. Just Observe, Relax and Let go. Observe for a duration of about 3 breaths.
26	Now move your awareness to your chest. Observe any sensations. Just Observe, Relax and Let go. Observe for a duration of about 3 breaths.
27	Now move your awareness to your upper belly. Observe any sensations. Just Observe, Relax and Let go. Observe for a duration of about 3 breaths.
28	Now move your awareness to your lower belly. Observe any sensations. Just Observe, Relax and Let go. Observe for a duration of about 3 breaths.
29	Now move your awareness to your left fingers and palm. Observe any sensations. Just Observe, Relax and Let go. Observe for a duration of about 3 breaths.
30	Now move your awareness to your left forearm. Observe any sensations. Just Observe, Relax and Let go. Observe for a duration of about 3 breaths.
31	Now move your awareness to your left upper arm. Observe any sensations. Just Observe, Relax and Let go. Observe for a duration of about 3 breaths.
32	Now move your awareness to your left shoulder and armpit and left side trunk of your body. Observe any sensations. Just Observe, Relax and Let go. Observe for a duration of about 3 breaths.
33	Now move your awareness to your left chest and back. Observe any sensations. Just Observe, Relax and Let go. Observe for a duration of about 3 breaths.
34	Now move your awareness to your right chest and back. Observe any sensations. Just Observe, Relax and Let go. Observe for a duration of about 3 breaths.

35	Now move your awareness to your right shoulder, armpit and side trunk of your body. Observe any sensations. Just Observe, Relax and Let go. Observe for a duration of about 3 breaths.
36	Now move your awareness to your right forearm. Observe any sensations. Just Observe, Relax and Let go. Observe for a duration of about 3 breaths.
37	Now move your awareness to your right fingers and palm. Observe any sensations. Just Observe, Relax and Let go. Observe for a duration of about 3 breaths.

Notes and Variations:

1	It is advised to practice mindfulness breath meditation before the mindfulness body meditation. For example: practice mindfulness breath meditation for 5 minutes and mindfulness body meditation for 15 minutes.
2	It is advised to observe the sensation in the heart area with the emotion of appreciation, gratitude, care and compassion after finishing the meditation.
3	The above serves as a guideline. When one is familiar with this meditation, feel free to create your own sequence. The key is to cover all the body parts. Observe the sensation with a relaxed and neutral attitude. Just observe, relax and let go.
4	If there is any emotion, thought or sensation that arises, please ignore. Keep focusing on the observation of sensation in the body.
5	In the beginning, focus on the skin of the body when observing the body sensations. One can choose to observe the 3D volume space of the body when one becomes familiar with the process.
6	Create a script, record it and play it out with your own voice. You can play music along with it.

Chapter 8 Ex-20 PARTNER MINDFULNESS MEDITATION.

When one is familiar with Anapana meditation, one starts to notice that the breath flow is NOT the same among the left and right nostrils. Our breath flows indicates our emotional state deep within our unconscious being. We can use our partner as a facilitator to trigger our hidden emotional states. We can then observe these deep hidden emotional states indirectly via our breath flow.

1	The two partners sit 6-feet apart face-to-face and do the Anapana meditation for 10 minutes.
2	Keep a journal and record the sensations, emotions and thoughts during the session.
3	Pay attention to which nostril is the dominant nostril and has the better breath flow during the session.
4	The two partners sit about 3-feet apart face-to-face and do the Anapana meditation for 10 minutes.
5	Record the sensations, emotions and thoughts during the session in your journal.
6	Pay attention to which nostril is the dominant nostril and has the better breath flow during the session.
7	The two partners sit as close as possible to each other face-to-face and do the Anapana meditation for 10 minutes.
8	Record the sensations, emotions and thoughts during the session in your journal.
9	After the activities are done, compare notes with each other.
10	Have a big hug and feel each other's breath and heart beats for at least 5 minutes after the session.
11	Remember to look into your partner's eye and say "I am grateful to you for doing this activity with me"

Notes and Variations:

1	Experiment with a different sitting configuration. For example: Back to Back, Shoulder to Shoulder, or sitting spoon position.
2	Partners can co-create mindfulness meditation scripts. Example: one partner can play the bell, gongs or instructment you resonate with. The other partner can read out the script... Experiment with being in different roles.
3	One way to do this experiment is to lay with your partner side by side or in a laying down spoon position.
4	Your dominant nostril would change if you lay on the side of your dominant nostril that has better air flow.

5	Pay attention if laying side by side with your partner changes your dominant nostril quicker (or slower)?

Chapter 9 Ex-21 HUMAN-INTERNAL-PLANETARY-ORBIT

Many spiritual traditions say: "As Above so Below." Modern science observes that Mother Nature uses the idea of recursion and factuality to create most of its form. This means that a smaller subsystem has the structure and property of the whole system. Vedic tradition states that the life forms in our solar system are evolving while traveling through the Cosmos. This path of traveling is an orbi, centered around the cosmic sun. Taoist Tradition and Kriya Yoga tradition of Lahiri Mahasaya state that in the human body, there is a similar pattern of evolution. Kriya tradition says that this path is our spinal cord and brain. The Taoist tradition says that this path is the micro and macro orbit of the acupuncture meridian system. Instead of mother earth, the breath is our carrier in this orbit.

Interestingly, the cerebrospinal fluid travel rate is observed to be increased during deep rhythmic breathing. Dan Winter suggests that the traveling rate of cerebrospinal fluid can alter the size and strength of our bio-field and aura. He says that there is a correlation between the quantity and quality of bliss one can experience, and the size and strength of our biofield and aura. MRI studies and Craniosacral therapy shows that having our spinal fluid moving optimally is critical to have a happy mood. A blissful person is more than a happy person. We, the authors, believe that the main purpose of human existence is having bliss. Honestly, if we look deeply at ourselves and our motivation for all of our daily activities, what else is there? The final goal is always having Bliss. The authors have observed that the Taoist breathing of micro-orbit can indeed generate intense bliss, like that of a whole-body orgasm during sex. Taoist Master Mantak Chia has taught micro-orbit breathing for training of the sexual energy. The micro-orbit activities described are an adaptation of such from the authors' personal experience.

1	Sit comfortably on a chair or on the floor cross-legged. (See Image)
2	Put the tip of the tongue behind the back of the upper front teeth
3	Take a deep relaxed inhalation with your nose and for a duration of four seconds.
4	During the inhalation move the awareness from the bottom of the spine to the top of the head and squeeze youranal sphincter muscle like holding the urine or feces while evacuating.
5	Hold the inhale breath and put the awareness at the top of the head for one second.
6	Exhale by simply relaxing your jaw, mouth, tongue and lips for four seconds
7	Hold the breath without inhaling again for a duration for one second while holding the awareness in the Xia Dan Tian discussed in the previous chapter. Just a reminder: it is about a four-finger-width below the navel and deep within the body.
8	This is one cycle.
9	Do this for a minimum of 10 minutes.

Notes and Variations

1	You can use a breath training app to train the breathing rhythm.
2	You can adjust the ratio of inhale, exhale, inhale-hold and exhale-hold to find a ratio that feels the best for you. One idea is to use the square breath training in a Free diving trainer app.
3	After one is familiar with the process, one can make the count using the major acupuncture points on the spine during inhalation and the major acupuncture points on the front of the body during exhalation.
4	Inhale Governing channel on spine: Contracting Perineum, One: Tail Bone, Two: opposite navel, Three: opposite solar plexus, Four: point opposite heart, Five: opposite throat, Six: base of skull: Seven: Top of the head. Eight: Eyebrow center
5	Hold:Eyebrow center or Upper Dan Tien at top of your head.
6	Exhale: One: Throat, Two: Heart, Three Solar Plexus, Four: Navel, Five: Sex Organs.
7	Hold: Xia Dan Tien or Perineum
8	You don't need to hit all the listed acupuncture points.
9	is more important to have a comfortable breathing rhythm.
10	Example: hold for one second at each point. The listed points would be an inhalation of 8 seconds, inhale-hold for 1 second, exhalation of 5 seconds and empty-hold 1 second for a total of 15 seconds. Some people would find they need a shorter cycle.
11	Instead, one can just do 6 points, for example: Inhale: Tailbone, opposite of heart and top of skull and Exhale: Throat, Heart and Navel.
12	Experiment with finding a rhythm and the points that resonate with you.
13	Experiment with different hand mudras during this activity.

The partner micro-orbit is building upon the micro-orbit. The blissful sensation can be more intense than that of the solo one, especially partnering with someone compatible.

Chapter 9 Ex-22 INTERNAL ORBIT PARTNER PART TWO

1	Find two chairs and a table where the partners can sit face to face and very close. (See Photos)
2	The feet of each partner can be touched comfortably with minimal stretching.

3	The hands of each partner can be touched on the table comfortably with minimal stretching.
4	The right hand is on top and the left hand is on the bottom.
5	The feet of partners' are touching.
6	The right foot is on top and the left foot is on the bottom.
7	Close your eyes.
8	Each partner follows the instructions of the micro-orbit.
9	Do this activity together for a minimum of 10 minutes.
10	Have a big hug and feel each other's breath and heart beats for at least 5 minutes after the session.
11	Remember to look into your partner's eye and say "I am grateful to you for doing this activity with me"

Notes and Variations:

1	Look into each other's eyes.
2	You can do without the table and just have hands on each other's thighs or knees.
3	One can experiment with sword mudra, which is energy projecting. Simply connect the tips of the thumb, ring and little fingers while having the index and middle finger stretch out. Do it with the right hand, while the other partner grasps and holds mudra's index and middle fingers with the left hand. It signifies the gesture and is an energetic transmitter and receiver of a tantric copulation exercise.
4	Experiment with different Mudras with each partner and observe the effects. Example: Use Gyan Mudra with the stretch out fingers on the center of partner's palm. Use Shuyan Mudra and make the circle intertwined with each other's
5	Partners can put a crystal, dry flower petals or dry herbs such as cannabis between the palms and hold together between the palms.
6	Create one's own partner Micro-Orbit script using the framework of Micro-Orbit script.

Figure 39. Partners Micro Orbits with Hand Mudras

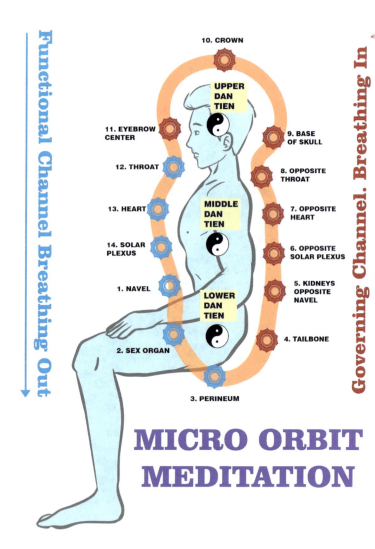

Figure 40. Major Energy Centers of Micro Orbit

Chapter 10 Ex-23 YOGIC FOOT GESTURE

1	Sit on the floor.
2	Make sure the spine is erected naturally.
3	Sit on a cushion to evaluate the hips if needed.
4	Right leg stretches out straight
5	The left leg bends and has the ankle touching the perineum.
6	Put the left hand on top of the stretch out right thigh, groin or knee.
7	Put the right hand on top of the left hand.
8	Inhale fully and put the awareness on the perineum and squeeze your anus.
9	Hold for the inhale breath for a duration that is comfortable for you.
10	Exhale, bend the torso comfortably as far as you can, but make sure the spine is naturally erected.
11	It's OK to bend just a little bit. It's all about quality and doing it RIGHT.
12	During the exhalation move the hands forward like rubbing your own legs from the top.
13	Empty, Hold and Return to the upright spine position.
14	Now, Switch the position of the hands.
15	The left hand is on the inside of the right upper thigh of the right leg
16	The right hand is on the outside of the right upper thigh of the left leg.
17	Inhale fully and put the awareness on the perineum and squeeze your anus.
18	Hold the inhale breath for a duration that is comfortable for you.
19	Exhale, bend the torso comfortably but make sure the spine is naturally erected.
20	During the exhalation, move the hands forward, like rubbing your own legs on the sides.
21	Inhale naturally and return to the upright spine position.
22	This is the sequence for the right leg.
23	Use a similar protocol for the left leg.
24	When both the left and right leg is done, this is counted as one cycle.
25	Make sure to do the same number of cycles on both legs.
26	It is suggested to do a minimum of three cycles on each leg. (See Images)

Chapter 10 Ex-24 YOGIC ROOT CHAKRA GESTURE

1	When one is familiar with the steps, one can experiment to put the awareness on the heart chakra or the third-eye chakra during exhalation.
2	One can experiment to have the bent leg in a kneeling position and sitting on the heel which is pressing the perineum.
3	By having the ankle or heel press the perineum, it increases the effectiveness

Chapter 10 Ex-25 PARTNER YOGIC LEG FOOT PLAY

The partner Mahamudra is building upon Mahamudra. Instead of rubbing one's own leg, one is rubbing your partner's leg. The idea is to massage each other's legs, feet and toes with synchronized breathing and movement together. The present of a partner can help accelerate the activation of the root energy vortex which is highly correlated to sex which is one of our prime survial instincts.

Follow these steps for Partner's Mahamudra. (See Photos & Images)

1	Partners face each other with Mahamudra position.
2	The straight leg of each partner is as close as possible to the private part of the other partner without touching the partner's private part. Your toes are able to touch your partner's private part if your foot is flexing out pointing.
3	Your bent leg's foot bottom should be touching your partner's straightened leg's outer calf or thigh, depending on the difference of leg length between partners.
4	Put the hands on the straight leg of the other partner. It can be on an ankle, calve, foot, toes or thigh.
5	Use the protocol of the Mahamudra discussed previously for breath and focus, but you are now using your partner's straightened leg instead. You are rubbing your partner's leg.
6	Synchronize the movement and breathing between the partners.
7	One partner can be the leader and call out the movement with the breathing.
8	Do your best NOT to push your foot onto your partner's private part.
9	Take turns to be the leader and the follower.
10	Have a big hug and feel each other's breath and heart beats for at least 5 minutes after the session.
11	Remember to look into your partner's eye and say "I am grateful to you for doing this activity with me".

Notes and Variations:

1	Partners can experiment with different hand and leg positions. Instead of rubbing legs, try grasping the calves or thighs and squeezing the calves or thighs.
2	You can put your fingers in your partner's toe webspace.
3	Sit side to side with each other and put the straight leg next to your partner's straight leg. Grab your partner's thigh or knee. Move sideways and attempt to touch your partner's thigh or knee with your forehead. Take Turns with the

	movement so as not to bang your heads against each others. Experiment with different breath Synchronization.
4	For example, when one partner is inhaling, the other partner is exhaling, or both partners inhale and exhale together.

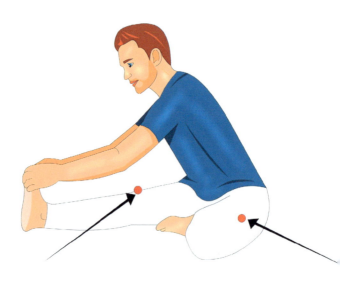

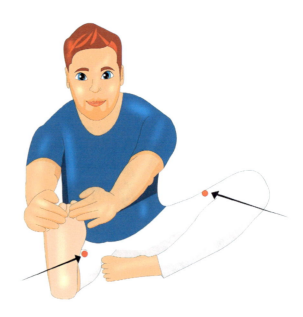

Figure 42. MahaMudra

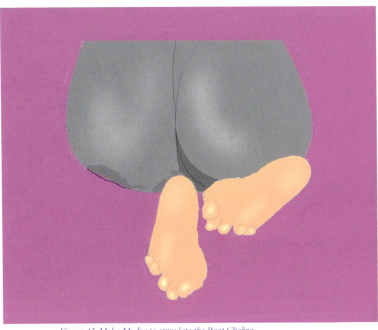

Figure 43. Maha Mudra to stimulate the Root Chakra

Figure 44. Partners Maha Mudras

Figure 45. Partners Maha Mudras

Figure 46. Partners Maha Mudra

12. Conclusion

Figure 47. Conscious BLissful Activies Without Sex

Life is a journey. We all know our final destination is DEATH, which we don't have control over. However, we have power over ourselves for how we treat our bodies, how we mind every moment and how we treat others during this journey.

As humans, we always strive for perfection, consciously or unconsciously. We want to become the best versions of ourselves and this gives us a great purpose in life. Perfection is different for each one of us. We should think of this story of evolution as the best movie in the whole universe. We can do it alone, or better yet, with a partner.

Let's recap. We covered the Mandala Gazing meditation that helps increase concentration with a focus on relaxed focus, and the Chakra meditation, which helps our cells to acquire new information.

Then comes breathing meditation and the body sensation meditation that increase self-awareness and reset our patterning. Tai Chi helps us to tune our biofield and expand our aura, especially when practicing outdoors. It also challenges us to have a relaxed focus with minimal effort, as Tai Chi is a form of standing and dynamic meditation

Other practices are Mantra chanting and singing to tone the bio-field with sound, and Hand Mudra Micro-Orbit and Mahamudras with the legs and feet, to help brain coordination.

Integration of all our roles in life is one of the keys to success during this human journey. How can we integrate and make this a congruent story?

Listening to what's deep inside is the first step for creating a coherent story. Sometimes, we get new ideas, but our bodies, which hold all the past memories, don't want to try this new idea, even if deep inside, we know it will be good for us if we act on this new idea. This is the beginning of the journey. Just show up and try a baby step. Showing up is the most important step. Have you ever postponed or even canceled your morning exercise routine because your body just wanted to lay in bed? Taking the first step, even if your habitual self does not want you to, can be the most challenging but it's the base of every new beginning.

Let's do our best to listen to that small inner voice and act on it to create the paths of re-creating our conscious and unconscious behaviors. You can choose mindless social media or shows for entertainment, you can choose to go out and party, or you can choose to stay home and practice the materials in this book with a partner or by yourself. Every human has the same number of hours per day, no matter who he or she is. The Universe isn't linear. You can do something simple and something extraordinary can happen. Dr. Joe Dispenza says, "the best way to predict our future is to create our own." You are the master and sole cause of your story.

A SUSTAINABLE PRACTICE FOR BOTH PARTNERS' MUTUAL GROWTH

Figure 48. Shareable Blissful Activities are required to acquire immortality according to Dan Winter
fractalfield.com

To build a successful and sustainable practice, we don't have to move mountains or challenge ourselves to walk popular trails around the world, like the Pacific Crest Trail. All we need to do is keep an open mind to new routines and be consistent.

It takes at least 30 days to change a habit. You don't even have to stress over this number if you do something small and be consistent each day with a partner. Keeping each other accountable goes a long way. When we begin a difficult journey along with someone, the hard part becomes less challenging. You and your partner will cheer each other on during low energy days.

Of course, remember to do what makes you and your partner both feel good. Find the most suitable and sustainable habit for it to be successful. Just like some people love cardio, others reap all the benefits from Pilates or yoga. One likes silent meditation practices, his or her partner may like singing mantras. Pick one or two solo practices and one partner practice that resonate with you and your partners the most, and stick with it for a period like 30 days or more. We encourage you to use this book as a framework and base, and then create your own routines and practice together. The practice routine will deepen and grow your relationship.

New habits can forge us into better versions of ourselves if we give them time. What's important is to also look into how having a healthy routine can help other areas of our lives too. For example, you start jogging daily to lose weight. Even if you don't lose the weight as you want, you become happier because of the routine exercise. When you are happy, you are more likely to be successful at other aspects of your life.

We are writing these out of LOVE. We believe what we share will help you and your partner have more bliss. We are writing out of our personal experience with each one of the above-mentioned activities. This is the "making of" a better you and your partner. It all starts with simple stuff. Simple mindful breathing when you feel stressed. Take a moment to feel your bodily sensations and the space around you before you sleep.

Your upgraded self can help brighten everybody you come in contact with. We pray that you and your partner join us on this journey that will help us bring more bliss and harmony toMother Earth.

Now use your most vibrant creative juice to write an implementable schedule for yourself and your partner of how you can up level yourself and your partner in the next 30 days. Spend at least 10 minutes and let your imagination go wild. Then go print it out and stick it somewhere obvious to remind you and your partner.

Resources

Anae Martin, Catherine, and Stéphane Cardinaux. *Structures vibratoires: des plans de conscience par les perceptions extrasensorielles, le ressenti corporel et les machines quantiques.* Éditions Trajectoire, 2018.

Buddhaghosa, Bhadantacariya. *The Path of Purification: Visuddhimagga.* Translated by Bhikkhu Nanamoli, Pariyatti Publishing, 2003.

Buttar, Rashid A. *The 9 Steps to Keep the Doctor Away: Simple Actions to Shift Your Body and Mind to Optimum Health for Greater Longevity.* GMEC Publishing, 2010.

Dispenza, Joe. *Becoming Supernatural: How Common People Are Doing the Uncommon.* Hay House, 2019.

Gergar, Lincoln. "Channel Higher Self." *Channel Higher Self - Higher Consciousness Spiritual Teachings & Guided Meditations Channel Higher Self,* https://channelhigherself.com/. Accessed 12 September 2022.

Goenka, S. N. *Satipatthana Sutta Discourses: Talks from a Course in Maha-satipatthana Sutta.* Edited by Patrick Given-Wilson, PARIYATTI PUB, 2020.

Hof, Wim. *The Wim Hof Method: Activate Your Full Human Potential.* Sounds True, 2020.

Iyengar, B. K. S. *Light on Yoga.* Schocken Books, 1995.

Jelusich, Richard. *Eye of the Lotus: Psychology of the Chakras.* Lotus Press, 2005.

Karim, Ibrahim. *BioGeometry Signatures: Harmonizing the Body's Subtle Energy Exchange with the Environment.* CreateSpace Independent Publishing Platform, 2016.

Mahasaya, Lahiri. *Kriya Yoga and Unlocking Mystical Songs of Kabir.* Createspace Independent Pub, 2013.

Motoyama, Hiroshi. *Karma and Reincarnation.* Edited by Rande Brown Ouchi, translated by Rande Brown Ouchi, Avon Books, 1993.

Paulsen, Norman. *Christ Consciousness: Emergence of the Pure Self Within.* Solar Logos Foundation, 2002.

Severinsen, Stig Åvall. *Breatheology: The Art of Conscious Breathing.* Idelson Gnocchi Pub, 2010.

Sharma, Shailendra. *Hatha Yoga Pradipika.* Shailendra Sharma, 2013.

Vimalarai, Bhante. *El Anapanasati Sutta: Desde Los Primeros Escritos De Buda / Early Writings from the Buddha.* Createspace Independent Pub, 2014.

Wangyal, Tenzin. *The Tibetan Yogas Of Dream And Sleep.* Edited by Mark Dahlby, Shambhala, 1998.

Winn, Michael, and Mantak Chia. *Taoist Secrets of Love: Cultivating Male Sexual Energy.* Aurora Press, 1984.

Winter, Dan. *Negentropic Fields: Announcements from Implosion Group- Dan Winter*, 2022, http://fractalfield.com. Accessed 12 September 2022.

Made in the USA
Columbia, SC
25 April 2025

57141543R00087